The Poetry of Edgar Allan Poe

The Poetry of Edgar Allan Poe

This edition published in 2020 by Arcturus Publishing Limited
26/27 Bickels Yard, 151–153 Bermondsey Street,
London SE1 3HA

AD007499US

Printed in the UK

Contents

Introduction

Today, Poe is best remembered as a writer of gothic horror tales, but he was also a magazine editor, literary critic, inventor of the modern detective story and, first and foremost, a poet. In his lifetime, the work that earned him the greatest popular acclaim was his poem "The Raven," published in 1845.

Born in Boston in 1809, Poe died in hospital in 1849, four days after being found in a Baltimore public house in a state of delirium, unable to explain what had happened to him. On the day of his burial, a vitriolic obituary appeared in the *New York Tribune*, which claimed that "few would be grieved" by the poet's death. This slanderous obituary, later revealed to have been written by Rufus Griswold, a literary rival, cast Poe as a drunken and depraved madman. This defamatory description served to shape his public image and continues to feed into his mythos today.

Poe's life included more than its fair share of difficulty and death. His mother and father had died of tuberculosis by the time he was three. His brother Henry and his foster mother, Frances Allan—to whom he was very close—also died before Poe turned 22. Little wonder, then, that he was obsessed with death. After being orphaned Poe was taken in by the wealthy Allan family from Richmond, Virginia, though they never formally adopted him. Poe excelled at school and was convinced of his future as a poet by the age of 13. However, a fractious relationship with his foster father, gambling debts, and romantic disappointment caused him to cut ties and leave home to seek his fortune.

In 1835, Poe began his ten-year career as a magazine editor in Richmond, Philadelphia, and New York City, also working as a literary critic and publishing his own poems and short stories. His reputation grew as did the circulations of many of his magazines. The following year, he married his cousin Virginia and began to write some of his most famous stories, including "The Tell-Tale Heart" and "The Murders in the Rue Morgue."

Though his output was small—the majority of his poems are included in this collection—he published his first book, *Tamerlane and Other Poems*, aged 18. Two other collections followed. Many of his early poems were closely associated with the romantic poetry of his time. But as he matured, his themes of romantic love, loss, and death, often told through the eyes of a narrator, centered on the psyche of the main character. Some of his work is surreal, but works such as "To Helen," "Lenore," "The Raven," "The Bells," and "Annabel Lee" have themes and qualities of lasting interest for contemporary readers.

His wife's death in 1847 hit him hard. His struggles with depression and alcoholism grew worse and he stopped writing. Within two years, he was dead from what was described by the hospital as "acute congestion of the brain," though the actual cause of his death remains a mystery.

Poems

O, Tempora! O, Mores!

O, Times! O, Manners! It is my opinion
That you are changing sadly your dominion—
I mean the reign of manners hath long ceased,
For men have none at all, or bad at least;
And as for times, although 'tis said by many
The "good old times" were far the worst of any,
Of which sound doctrine I believe each tittle,
Yet still I think these worse than them a little.

I've been a thinking—isn't that the phrase?
—I like your Yankee words and Yankee ways—
I've been a thinking, whether it were best
To take things seriously, or all in jest;
Whether, with grim Heraclitus of yore,
To weep, as he did, till his eyes were sore,
Or rather laugh with him, that queer Philosopher,
Democritus of Thrace, who used to toss over
The page of life and grin at the dog-ears,
As though he'd say, "Why, who the devil cares?"

This is a question which, oh Heaven, withdraw
The luckless query from a Member's claw!
Instead of two sides, Bob has nearly eight,
Each fit to furnish forth four hours debate.
What shall be done? I'll lay it on the table,
And take the matter up when I'm more able,
And, in the meantime, to prevent all bother,
I'll neither laugh with one, nor cry with t'other,

Nor deal in flattery or aspersions foul,
But, taking one by each hand, merely growl.

Ah, growl, say you, my friend, and pray at what?
Why, really, sir, I almost had forgot—
But, damn it, sir, I deem it a disgrace
That things should stare us boldly in the face,
And daily strut the street with bows and scrapes,
Who would be men by imitating apes.
I beg your pardon, reader, for the oath
The monkeys make me swear, though something loath;
I'm apt to be discursive in my style,
But pray be patient: yet a little while
Will change me, and as politicians do,
I'll mend my manners and my measures too.

Of all the cities—and I've seen no few;
For I have travelled, friend, as well as you—
I don't remember one, upon my soul,
But take it generally upon the whole,
(As Members say they like their logic taken,
Because divided, it may chance be shaken)
So pat, agreeable and vastly proper
As this for a neat, frisky counter-hopper;
Here he may revel to his heart's content,
Flounce like a fish in his own element,
Toss back his fine curls from their forehead fair,
And hop o'er counters with a Vestris air,
Complete at night what he began A.M.,
And having cheated ladies, dance with them;
For, at a ball, what fair one can escape
The pretty little hand that sold her tape,

Or who so cold, so callous to refuse
The youth who cut the ribbon for her shoes!

One of these fish, par excellence the beau,
God help me, it has been my lot to know,
At least by sight, for I'm a timid man,
And always keep from laughing, if I can;
But speak to him, he'll make you such grimace,
Lord! to be grave exceeds the power of face.
The hearts of all the ladies are with him,
Their bright eyes on his Tom and Jerry brim
And dove-tailed coat, obtained at cost; while then
Those eyes won't turn on anything like men.

His very voice is musical delight,
His form, once seen, becomes a part of sight;
In short, his shirt collar, his look, his tone is
The "beau ideal" fancied for Adonis.
Philosophers have often held dispute
As to the seat of thought in man and brute;
For that the power of thought attends the latter
My friend, the beau, hath made a settled matter,
And spite of all dogmas current in all ages,
One settled fact is better than ten sages.

For he does think, though I'm oft in doubt
If I can tell exactly what about.
Ah, yes! his little foot and ankle trim,
'Tis there the seat of reason lies in him,
A wise philosopher would shake his head,
He then, of course, must shake his foot instead.
At me, in vengeance, shall that foot be shaken—

Another proof of thought, I'm not mistaken—
Because to his cat's eyes I hold a glass,
And let him see himself, a proper ass!
I think he'll take this likeness to himself,
But if he won't he shall, a stupid elf,
And, lest the guessing throw the fool in fits,
I close the portrait with the name of Pitts.

Song

I saw thee on thy bridal day—
    When a burning blush came o'er thee,
Though happiness around thee lay,
    The world all love before thee:

And in thine eye a kindling light
    (Whatever it might be)
Was all on Earth my aching sight
    Of Loveliness could see.

That blush, perhaps, was maiden shame—
    As such it well may pass—
Though its glow hath raised a fiercer flame
    In the breast of him, alas!

Who saw thee on that bridal day,
    When that deep blush *would* come o'er thee,
Though happiness around thee lay,
    The world all love before thee.

The Lake: To ——

In spring of youth it was my lot
To haunt of the wide earth a spot
The which I could not love the less—
So lovely was the loneliness
Of a wild lake, with black rock bound,
And the tall pines that towered around.

But when the Night had thrown her pall
Upon that spot, as upon all,
And the mystic wind went by
Murmuring in melody—
Then—ah, then—I would awake
To the terror of the lone lake.

Yet that terror was not fright,
But a tremulous delight—
A feeling not the jewelled mine
Could teach or bribe me to define—
Nor Love—although the Love were thine.

Death was in that poisonous wave,
And in its gulf a fitting grave
For him who thence could solace bring
To his lone imagining—
Whose solitary soul could make
An Eden of that dim lake.

Imitation

A dark unfathomed tide
Of interminable pride—
A mystery, and a dream,
Should my early life seem;
I say that dream was fraught
With a wild and waking thought
Of beings that have been,
Which my spirit hath not seen,
Had I let them pass me by,
With a dreaming eye!
Let none of earth inherit
That vision on my spirit;
Those thoughts I would control,
As a spell upon his soul:
For that bright hope at last
And that light time have past,
And my wordly rest hath gone
With a sigh as it passed on:
I care not though it perish
With a thought I then did cherish.

The Happiest Day

The happiest day—the happiest hour
    My sear'd and blighted heart hath known,
The highest hope of pride and power,
    I feel hath flown.

Of power! said I? yes! such I ween
    But they have vanish'd long, alas!
The visions of my youth have been—
    But let them pass.

And pride, what have I now with thee?
    Another brow may ev'n inherit
The venom thou hast pour'd on me—
    Be still, my spirit!

The happiest day—the happiest hour
    Mine eyes shall see—have ever seen,
The brightest glance of pride and power
    I feel—have been:

But were that hope of pride and power
    Now offer'd with the pain
Ev'n then I felt—that brightest hour
    I would not live again:

For on its wing was dark alloy
    And as it flutter'd—fell
An essence—powerful to destroy
    A soul that knew it well.

Evening Star

'Twas noontide of summer,
    And mid-time of night;
And stars, in their orbits,
    Shone pale, thro' the light
Of the brighter, cold moon.
    'Mid planets her slaves,
Herself in the Heavens,
    Her beam on the waves.
    I gaz'd awhile
    On her cold smile;
Too cold—too cold for me—
    There pass'd as a shroud,
    A fleecy cloud,
And I turn'd away to thee,
    Proud Evening Star,
    In thy glory afar
And dearer thy beam shall be;
    For joy to my heart
    Is the proud part
Thou bearest in Heav'n at night,
    And more I admire
    Thy distant fire
Than that colder, lowly light.

Hymn to Aristogeiton and Harmodius

I

Wreathed in myrtle, my sword I'll conceal,
Like those champions devoted and brave,
When they plunged in the tyrant their steel,
And to Athens deliverance gave.

II

Beloved heroes! your deathless souls roam
In the joy breathing isles of the blest;
Where the mighty of old have their home—
Where Achilles and Diomed rest.

III

In fresh myrtle my blade I'll entwine,
Like Harmodius, the gallant and good,
When he made at the tutelar shrine
A libation of Tyranny's blood.

IV

Ye deliverers of Athens from shame!
Ye avengers of Liberty's wrongs!
Endless ages shall cherish your fame,
Embalmed in their echoing songs!

Dreams

Oh! that my young life were a lasting dream!
My spirit not awak'ning, till the beam
Of an Eternity should bring the morrow.
Yes! tho' that long dream were of hopeless sorrow,
'Twere better than the cold reality
Of waking life, to him whose heart must be,
And hath been still, upon the lovely earth,
A chaos of deep passion, from his birth.
But should it be—that dream eternally
Continuing—as dreams have been to me
In my young boyhood—should it thus be giv'n,
'Twere folly still to hope for higher Heav'n.
For I have revell'd when the sun was bright
I' the summer sky, in dreams of living light
And loveliness,—have left my very heart
In climes of mine imagining, apart
From mine own home, with beings that have been
Of mine own thought—what more could I have seen?
'Twas once—and only once—and the wild hour
From my remembrance shall not pass—some pow'r
Or spell had bound me—'twas the chilly wind
Came o'er me in the night, and left behind
Its image on my spirit—or the moon
Shone on my slumbers in her lofty noon
Too coldly—or the stars—howe'er it was
That dream was that that night-wind—let it pass.
I *have been* happy, tho' in a dream.
I have been happy—and I love the theme:
Dreams! in their vivid coloring of life
As in that fleeting, shadowy, misty strife

Of semblance with reality which brings
To the delirious eye, more lovely things
Of Paradise and Love—and all my own!—
Than young Hope in his sunniest hour hath known.

In Youth I Have Known One

How often we forget all time, when lone
Admiring Nature's universal throne;
Her woods—her wilds—her mountains—the intense
Reply of Hers to Our intelligence!

I

In youth I have known one with whom the Earth
　　In secret communing held—as he with it,
In daylight, and in beauty, from his birth:
　　Whose fervid, flickering torch of life was lit
From the sun and stars, whence he had drawn forth
　　A passionate light such for his spirit was fit—
And yet that spirit knew—not in the hour
　　Of its own fervor—what had o'er it power.

II

Perhaps it may be that my mind is wrought
　　To a fever by the moonbeam that hangs o'er,
But I will half believe that wild light fraught
　　With more of sovereignty than ancient lore
Hath ever told—or is it of a thought
　　The unembodied essence, and no more
That with a quickening spell doth o'er us pass
　　As dew of the night-time, o'er the summer grass?

III

Doth o'er us pass, when, as th' expanding eye
　　To the loved object—so the tear to the lid
Will start, which lately slept in apathy?
　　And yet it need not be—(that object) hid

From us in life—but common—which doth lie
 Each hour before us—but then only bid
With a strange sound, as of a harp-string broken
 T' awake us—'Tis a symbol and a token—

IV

Of what in other worlds shall be—and given
 In beauty by our God, to those alone
Who otherwise would fall from life and Heaven
 Drawn by their heart's passion, and that tone,
That high tone of the spirit which hath striven
 Though not with Faith—with godliness—whose
  throne
With desperate energy 't hath beaten down;
 Wearing its own deep feeling as a crown.

A Pæan

I

How shall the burial rite be read?
    The solemn song be sung?
The requiem for the loveliest dead,
    That ever died so young?

II

Her friends are gazing on her,
    And on her gaudy bier,
And weep!—oh! to dishonor
    Dead beauty with a tear!

III

They loved her for her wealth—
    And they hated her for her pride—
But she grew in feeble health,
    And they *love* her—that she died.

IV

They tell me (while they speak
    Of her "costly broider'd pall")
That my voice is growing weak—
    That I should not sing at all—

V

Or that my tone should be
    Tun'd to such solemn song
So mournfully—so mournfully,
    That the dead may feel no wrong.

VI

But she is gone above,
  With young Hope at her side,
And I am drunk with love
  Of the dead, who is my bride.—

VII

Of the dead—dead who lies
  All perfum'd there,
With the death upon her eyes.
  And the life upon her hair.

VIII

Thus on the coffin loud and long
  I strike—the murmur sent
Through the gray chambers to my song,
  Shall be the accompaniment.

IX

Thou dieds't in thy life's June—
  But thou didst not die too fair:
Thou didst not die too soon,
  Nor with too calm an air.

X

From more than friends on earth,
  Thy life and love are riven,
To join the untainted mirth
  Of more than thrones in heaven.—

XI

Therefore, to thee this night
    I will no requiem raise,
But waft thee on thy flight,
    With a Pæan of old days.

Romance

Romance, who loves to nod and sing,
With drowsy head and folded wing,
Among the green leaves as they shake
Far down within some shadowy lake,
To me a painted paroquet
Hath been—a most familiar bird—
Taught me my alphabet to say—
To lisp my very earliest word
While in the wild wood I did lie,
A child—with a most knowing eye.

Of late, eternal Condor years
So shake the very Heaven on high
With tumult as they thunder by,
I have no time for idle cares
Through gazing on the unquiet sky.
And when an hour with calmer wings
Its down upon my spirit flings—
That little time with lyre and rhyme
To while away—forbidden things!
My heart would feel to be a crime
Unless it trembled with the strings.

Sonnet—to Science

Science! true daughter of Old Time thou art!
    Who alterest all things with thy peering eyes.
Why preyest thou thus upon the poet's heart,
    Vulture, whose wings are dull realities?
How should he love thee? or how deem thee wise,
    Who wouldst not leave him in his wandering
To seek for treasure in the jewelled skies,
    Albeit he soared with an undaunted wing?
Hast thou not dragged Diana from her car?
    And driven the Hamadryad from the wood
To seek a shelter in some happier star?
    Hast thou not torn the Naiad from her flood,
The Elfin from the green grass, and from me
The summer dream beneath the tamarind tree?

An Acrostic

Elizabeth it is in vain you say
"Love not"—thou sayest it in so sweet a way:
In vain those words from thee or L. E. L.
Zantippe's talents had enforced so well:
Ah! if that language from thy heart arise,
Breathe it less gently forth—and veil thine eyes.
Endymion, recollect, when Luna tried
To cure his love—was cured of all beside—
His follie—pride—and passion—for he died.

To ——

I heed not that my earthly lot
    Hath—little of Earth in it—
That years of love have been forgot
    In the hatred of a minute:—
I mourn not that the desolate
    Are happier, sweet, than I,
But that you sorrow for my fate
    Who am a passer-by.

To ——

The bowers whereat, in dreams, I see
    The wantonest singing birds,
Are lips—and all thy melody
    Of lip-begotten words.

Thine eyes, in Heaven of heart enshrined
    Then desolately fall,
O God! on my funereal mind
    Like starlight on a pall.

Thy heart—thy heart!—I wake and sigh,
    And sleep to dream till day
Of the truth that gold can never buy—
    Of the baubles that it may.

Alone

From childhood's hour I have not been
As others were—I have not seen
As others saw—I could not bring
My passions from a common spring—
From the same source I have not taken
My sorrow—I could not awaken
My heart to joy at the same tone—
And all I lov'd—*I* lov'd alone—
Then—in my childhood—in the dawn
Of a most stormy life—was drawn
From ev'ry depth of good and ill
The mystery which binds me still—
From the torrent, or the fountain—
From the red cliff of the mountain—
From the sun that 'round me roll'd
In its autumn tint of gold—
From the lightning in the sky
As it pass'd me flying by—
From the thunder, and the storm—
And the cloud that took the form
(When the rest of Heaven was blue)
Of a demon in my view.

Elizabeth

Elizabeth—it surely is most fit
    (Logic and common usage so commanding)
In thy own book that *first* thy name be writ,
    Zeno and other sages notwithstanding:
And I have other reasons for so doing
    Besides my innate love of contradiction:
Each poet—*if* a poet—in pursuing
    The muses thro' their bowers of Truth or Fiction,
Has studied very little of his part,
    Read nothing, written less—in short's a fool
Endued with neither soul, nor sense, nor art,
    Being ignorant of one important rule,
Employed in even the theses of the school—
    Called——I forget the heathenish Greek name
(Called anything, its meaning is the same)
    "Always write *first* things uppermost in the heart."

Tamerlane

Kind solace in a dying hour!
    Such, father, is not (now) my theme—
I will not madly deem that power
      Of Earth may shrive me of the sin
      Unearthly pride hath revel'd in—
    I have no time to dote or dream:
You call it hope—that fire of fire!
It is but agony of desire:
If I *can* hope—Oh God! I can—
    Its fount is holier—more divine—
I would not call thee fool, old man,
    But such is not a gift of thine.

Know thou the secret of a spirit
    Bow'd from its wild pride into shame.
O yearning heart! I did inherit
    Thy withering portion with the fame,
The searing glory which hath shone
Amid the jewels of my throne,
Halo of Hell! and with a pain
Not Hell shall make me fear again—
O craving heart, for the lost flowers
And sunshine of my summer hours!
The undying voice of that dead time,
With its interminable chime,
Rings, in the spirit of a spell,
Upon thy emptiness—a knell.

I have not always been as now:
The fever'd diadem on my brow

I claim'd and won usurpingly—
Hath not the same fierce heirdom given
  Rome to the Cæsar—this to me?
    The heritage of a kingly mind,
And a proud spirit which hath striven
    Triumphantly with human kind.

On mountain soil I first drew life:
    The mists of the Taglay have shed
    Nightly their dews upon my head,
And, I believe, the winged strife
And tumult of the headlong air
Have nestled in my very hair.

So late from Heaven—that dew—it fell
    ('Mid dreams of an unholy night)
Upon me with the touch of Hell,
    While the red flashing of the light
From clouds that hung, like banners, o'er,
    Appeared to my half-closing eye
    The pageantry of monarchy,
And the deep trumpet-thunder's roar
    Came hurriedly upon me, telling
    Of human battle, where my voice,
    My own voice, silly child!—was swelling
    (O! how my spirit would rejoice,
And leap within me at the cry)
The battle-cry of Victory!

The rain came down upon my head
    Unshelter'd—and the heavy wind

Rendered me mad and deaf and blind.
It was but man, I thought, who shed
    Laurels upon me: and the rush—
    The torrent of the chilly air
Gurgled within my ear the crush
    Of empires—with the captive's prayer—
The hum of suitors—and the tone
Of flattery 'round a sovereign's throne.

My passions, from that hapless hour,
    Usurp'd a tyranny which men
Have deem'd, since I have reach'd to power,
      My innate nature—be it so:
    But, father, there liv'd one who, then,
Then—in my boyhood—when their fire
      Burn'd with a still intenser glow,
(For passion must, with youth, expire)
    E'en *then* who knew this iron heart
    In woman's weakness had a part.

I have no words—alas!—to tell
The loveliness of loving well!
Nor would I now attempt to trace
The more than beauty of a face
Whose lineaments, upon my mind,
Are——shadows on th' unstable wind:
Thus I remember having dwelt
    Some page of early lore upon,
With loitering eye, till I have felt
The letters—with their meaning—melt
    To fantasies—with none.

O, she was worthy of all love!
　　Love—as in infancy was mine—
'Twas such as angel minds above
　　Might envy; her young heart the shrine
On which my every hope and thought
　　Were incense—then a goodly gift,
　　　For they were childish and upright—
Pure——as her young example taught:
　　Why did I leave it, and, adrift,
　　　Trust to the fire within, for light?

We grew in age—and love—together—
　　Roaming the forest, and the wild;
My breast her shield in wintry weather—
　　And, when the friendly sunshine smil'd,
And she would mark the opening skies,
I saw no Heaven—but in her eyes.

Young Love's first lesson is——the heart:
　　For 'mid that sunshine, and those smiles,
When, from our little cares apart,
　　And laughing at her girlish wiles,
I'd throw me on her throbbing breast,
　　And pour my spirit out in tears—
There was no need to speak the rest—
　　No need to quiet any fears
Of her—who ask'd no reason why,
But turn'd on me her quiet eye!

Yet more than worthy of the love
My spirit struggled with, and strove,
When, on the mountain peak, alone,

Ambition lent it a new tone—
I had no being—but in thee:
    The world, and all it did contain
In the earth—the air—the sea—
    Its joy—its little lot of pain
That was new pleasure——the ideal,
    Dim, vanities of dreams by night—
And dimmer nothings which were real—
    (Shadows—and a more shadowy light!)
Parted upon their misty wings,
        And, so, confusedly, became
        Thine image, and—a name—a name!
Two separate—yet most intimate things.

I was ambitious—have you known
    The passion, father? You have not:
A cottager, I mark'd a throne
Of half the world as all my own,
    And murmur'd at such lowly lot—
But, just like any other dream,
    Upon the vapor of the dew
My own had past, did not the beam
    Of beauty which did while it thro'
The minute—the hour—the day—oppress
My mind with double loveliness.

We walk'd together on the crown
Of a high mountain which look'd down
Afar from its proud natural towers
    Of rock and forest, on the hills—
The dwindled hills! begirt with bowers
    And shouting with a thousand rills.

I spoke to her of power and pride,
But mystically—in such guise
That she might deem it nought beside
The moment's converse; in her eyes
I read, perhaps too carelessly—
A mingled feeling with my own—
The flush on her bright cheek, to me
Seem'd to become a queenly throne
Too well that I should let it be
Light in the wilderness alone.

I wrapp'd myself in grandeur then,
And donn'd a visionary crown——
Yet it was not that Fantasy
Had thrown her mantle over me—
But that, among the rabble—men,
Lion ambition is chain'd down—
And crouches to a keeper's hand—
Not so in deserts where the grand—
The wild—the terrible conspire
With their own breath to fan his fire.

Look 'round thee now on Samarcand!—
Is not she queen of Earth? her pride
Above all cities? in her hand
Their destinies? in all beside
Of glory which the world hath known
Stands she not nobly and alone?
Falling—her veriest stepping-stone
Shall form the pedestal of a throne—
And who her sovereign? Timour—he
Whom the astonished people saw

Striding o'er empires haughtily
    A diadem'd outlaw!

O, human love! thou spirit given,
On Earth, of all we hope in Heaven!
Which fall'st into the soul like rain
Upon the Siroc-wither'd plain,
And, failing in thy power to bless,
But leav'st the heart a wilderness!
Idea! which bindest life around
With music of so strange a sound
And beauty of so wild a birth—
Farewell! for I have won the Earth!

When Hope, the eagle that tower'd, could see
    No cliff beyond him in the sky,
His pinions were bent droopingly—
    And homeward turn'd his soften'd eye.
'Twas sunset: when the sun will part
There comes a sullenness of heart
To him who still would look upon
The glory of the summer sun.
That soul will hate the ev'ning mist
So often lovely, and will list
To the sound of the coming darkness (known
To those whose spirits hearken) as one
Who, in a dream of night, would fly
But cannot from a danger nigh.

What tho' the moon—the white moon
Shed all the splendor of her noon,
Her smile is chilly—and her beam,

In that time of dreariness, will seem
(So like you gather in your breath)
A portrait taken after death.
And boyhood is a summer sun
Whose waning is the dreariest one.
For all we live to know is known,
And all we seek to keep hath flown.
Let life, then, as the day-flower, fall
With the noon-day beauty—which is all.

I reach'd my home—my home no more—
　　　For all had flown who made it so.
I pass'd from out its mossy door,
　　　And, tho' my tread was soft and low,
A voice came from the threshold stone
Of one whom I had earlier known—
　　　O, I defy thee, Hell, to show
　　　On beds of fire that burn below,
　　　An humbler heart—a deeper woe.

Father, I firmly do believe—
　　　I know—for Death who comes for me
　　　From regions of the blest afar,
Where there is nothing to deceive,
　　　Hath left his iron gate ajar,
　　　And rays of truth you cannot see
　　　Are flashing thro' Eternity—
I do believe that Eblis hath
A snare in every human path—
Else how, when in the holy grove
I wandered of the idol, Love,
Who daily scents his snowy wings

With incense of burnt offerings
From the most unpolluted things,
Whose pleasant bowers are yet so riven
Above with trellis'd rays from Heaven
No mote may shun—no tiniest fly
The light'ning of his eagle eye—
How was it that Ambition crept,
    Unseen, amid the revels there,
Till growing bold, he laughed and leapt
    In the tangles of Love's very hair?

To Isadore

I

Beneath the vine-clad eaves,
    Whose shadows fall before
    Thy lowly cottage door—
Under the lilac's tremulous leaves—
Within thy snowy clasped hand
    The purple flowers it bore.
Last eve in dreams, I saw thee stand,
Like queenly nymph from Fairy-land—
Enchantress of the flowery wand,
    Most beauteous Isadore!

II

And when I bade the dream
    Upon thy spirit flee,
    Thy violet eyes to me
Upturned, did overflowing seem
With the deep, untold delight
    Of Love's serenity;
Thy classic brow, like lilies white
And pale as the Imperial Night
Upon her throne, with stars bedight,
    Enthralled my soul to thee!

III

Ah! ever I behold
    Thy dreamy, passionate eyes,
    Blue as the languid skies
Hung with the sunset's fringe of gold;
Now strangely clear thine image grows,

And olden memories
Are startled from their long repose
Like shadows on the silent snows
When suddenly the night-wind blows
  Where quiet moonlight lies.

IV

Like music heard in dreams,
  Like strains of harps unknown,
  Of birds for ever flown—
Audible as the voice of streams
That murmur in some leafy dell,
  I hear thy gentlest tone,
And Silence cometh with her spell
Like that which on my tongue doth dwell,
When tremulous in dreams I tell
  My love to thee alone!

V

In every valley heard,
  Floating from tree to tree,
  Less beautiful to me,
The music of the radiant bird,
Than artless accents such as thine
  Whose echoes never flee!
Ah! how for thy sweet voice I pine:—
For uttered in thy tones benign
(Enchantress!) this rude name of mine
  Doth seem a melody!

The Village Street

In these rapid, restless shadows,
       Once I walked at eventide,
When a gentle, silent maiden,
       Walked in beauty at my side.
She alone there walked beside me
       All in beauty, like a bride.

Pallidly the moon was shining
       On the dewy meadows nigh;
On the silvery, silent rivers,
       On the mountains far and high,—
On the ocean's star-lit waters,
       Where the winds a-weary die.

Slowly, silently we wandered
       From the open cottage door,
Underneath the elm's long branches
       To the pavement bending o'er;
Underneath the mossy willow
       And the dying sycamore.

With the myriad stars in beauty
       All bedight, the heavens were seen,
Radiant hopes were bright around me,
       Like the light of stars serene;
Like the mellow midnight splendor
       Of the Night's irradiate queen.

Audibly the elm-leaves whispered
       Peaceful, pleasant melodies,

Like the distant murmured music
　　Of unquiet, lovely seas;
While the winds were hushed in slumber
　　In the fragrant flowers and trees.

Wondrous and unwonted beauty
　　Still adorning all did seem,
While I told my love in fables
　　'Neath the willows by the stream;
Would the heart have kept unspoken
　　Love that was its rarest dream!

Instantly away we wandered
　　In the shadowy twilight tide,
She, the silent, scornful maiden,
　　Walking calmly at my side,
With a step serene and stately,
　　All in beauty, all in pride.

Vacantly I walked beside her.
　　On the earth mine eyes were cast;
Swift and keen there came unto me
　　Bitter memories of the past—
On me, like the rain in Autumn
　　On the dead leaves, cold and fast.

Underneath the elms we parted,
　　By the lowly cottage door;
One brief word alone was uttered—
　　Never on our lips before;
And away I walked forlornly,
　　Broken-hearted evermore.

Slowly, silently I loitered,
    Homeward, in the night, alone;
Sudden anguish bound my spirit,
    That my youth had never known;
Wild unrest, like that which cometh
    When the Night's first dream hath flown.

Now, to me the elm-leaves whisper
    Mad, discordant melodies,
And keen melodies like shadows
    Haunt the moaning willow trees,
And the sycamores with laughter
    Mock me in the nightly breeze.

Sad and pale the Autumn moonlight
    Through the sighing foliage streams;
And each morning, midnight shadow,
    Shadow of my sorrow seems;
Strive, O heart, forget thine idol!
    And, O soul, forget thy dreams!

The Forest Reverie

'Tis said that when
The hands of men
Tamed this primeval wood,
And hoary trees with groans of woe,
Like warriors by an unknown foe,
Were in their strength subdued,
The virgin Earth
Gave instant birth
To springs that ne'er did flow—
That in the sun
Did rivulets run,
And all around rare flowers did blow—
The wild rose pale
Perfumed the gale
And the queenly lily adown the dale
(Whom the sun and the dew
And the winds did woo),
With the gourd and the grape luxuriant grew.

So when in tears
The love of years
Is wasted like the snow,
And the fine fibrils of its life
By the rude wrong of instant strife
Are broken at a blow—
Within the heart
Do springs upstart
Of which it doth now know,
And strange, sweet dreams,

Like silent streams
That from new fountains overflow,
With the earlier tide
Of rivers glide
Deep in the heart whose hope has died—
Quenching the fires its ashes hide,—
Its ashes, whence will spring and grow
Sweet flowers, ere long,—
The rare and radiant flowers of song!

To the River

Fair river! in thy bright, clear flow
    Of crystal, wandering water,
Thou art an emblem of the glow
      Of beauty—the unhidden heart—
      The playful maziness of art
    In old Alberto's daughter;
But when within thy wave she looks—
    Which glistens then, and trembles—
Why, then, the prettiest of brooks
    Her worshipper resembles;
For in his heart, as in thy stream,
    Her image deeply lies—
His heart which trembles at the beam
    Of her soul-searching eyes.

Fairy-Land

Dim vales—and shadowy floods—
And cloudy-looking woods,
Whose forms we can't discover
For the tears that drip all over:
Huge moons there wax and wane—
Again—again—again—
Every moment of the night—
Forever changing places—
And they put out the star-light
With the breath from their pale faces.
About twelve by the moon-dial
One more filmy than the rest
(A kind which, upon trial,
They have found to be the best)
Comes down—still down—and down
With its centre on the crown
Of a mountain's eminence,
While its wide circumference
In easy drapery falls
Over hamlets, over halls,
Wherever they may be—
O'er the strange woods—o'er the sea—
Over spirits on the wing—
Over every drowsy thing—
And buries them up quite
In a labyrinth of light—
And then, how deep!—O, deep!
Is the passion of their sleep.
In the morning they arise,

And their moony covering
Is soaring in the skies,
With the tempests as they toss,
Like—almost any thing—
Or a yellow Albatross.
They use that moon no more
For the same end as before—
Videlicet, a tent—
Which I think extravagant:
Its atomies, however,
Into a shower dissever,
Of which those butterflies,
Of Earth, who seek the skies,
And so come down again
(Never-contented thing!)
Have brought a specimen
Upon their quivering wings.

The Valley of Unrest

Once it smiled a silent dell
Where the people did not dwell;
They had gone unto the wars,
Trusting to the mild-eyed stars,
Nightly, from their azure towers,
To keep watch above the flowers,
In the midst of which all day
The red sun-light lazily lay.
Now each visitor shall confess
The sad valley's restlessness.
Nothing there is motionless—
Nothing save the airs that brood
Over the magic solitude.
Ah, by no wind are stirred those trees
That palpitate like the chill seas
Around the misty Hebrides!
Ah, by no wind those clouds are driven
That rustle through the unquiet Heaven
Uneasily, from morn till even,
Over the violets there that lie
In myriad types of the human eye—
Over the lilies there that wave
And weep above a nameless grave!
They wave:—from out their fragrant tops
Eternal dews come down in drops.
They weep:—from off their delicate stems
Perennial tears descend in gems.

To Helen

Helen, thy beauty is to me
    Like those Nicèan barks of yore,
That gently, o'er a perfumed sea,
    The weary way-worn wanderer bore
    To his own native shore.

On desperate seas long wont to roam,
    Thy hyacinth hair, thy classic face,
Thy Naiad airs have brought me home
    To the glory that was Greece,
And the grandeur that was Rome.

Lo! in yon brilliant window-niche
    How statue-like I see thee stand,
    The agate lamp within thy hand!
Ah, Psyche, from the regions which
    Are Holy-land!

Lenore

Ah, broken is the golden bowl!—the spirit flown forever!
Let the bell toll!—a saintly soul floats on the Stygian river;
And, Guy De Vere, hast thou no tear?—weep now or never
    more!
See! on yon drear and rigid bier low lies thy love, Lenore!
Come! let the burial rite be read—the funeral song be
    sung!—
An anthem for the queenliest dead that ever died so
    young—
A dirge for her the doubly dead in that she died so
    young.

"Wretches! ye loved her for her wealth, and ye hated her
    for her pride,
And when she fell in feeble health, ye blessed her—that
    she died:—
How shall the ritual, then, be read—the requiem how be
    sung
By you—by yours, the evil eye,—by yours, the slanderous
    tongue
That did to death the innocence that died, and died so
    young?"

Peccavimus; but rave not thus! but let a Sabbath song
Go up to God so solemnly the dead may feel no wrong!
The sweet Lenore hath gone before, with Hope, that flew
    beside,
Leaving thee wild for the dear child that should have been
    thy bride—
For her, the fair and debonair, that now so lowly lies,

The life upon her yellow hair, but not within her eyes—
The life still there upon her hair, the death upon her eyes.

"Avaunt!—avaunt! to friends from fiends the indignant
    ghost is riven—
From Hell unto a high estate within the utmost Heaven—
From moan and groan to a golden throne beside the king
    of Heaven:—
Let no bell toll, then, lest her soul, amid its hallowed
    mirth,
Should catch the note as it doth float up from the
    damnèd Earth!
And I—tonight my heart is light:—no dirge will I
    upraise,
But waft the angel on her flight with a Pæan of old
    days!"

Fanny

The dying swan by northern lakes
    Sings its wild death song, sweet and clear,
And as the solemn music breaks
    O'er hill and glen dissolves in air;
Thus musical thy soft voice came,
Thus trembled on thy tongue my name.
Like sunburst through the ebon cloud,
    Which veils the solemn midnight sky,
Piercing cold evening's sable shroud,
    Thus came the first glance of that eye;
But like the adamantine rock,
My spirit met and braved the shock.
Let memory the boy recall
    Who laid his heart upon thy shrine,
When far away his footsteps fall,
    Think that he deem'd thy charms divine;
A victim on love's altar slain,
By witching eyes which looked disdain.

TAMERLANE

Serenade

So sweet the hour—so calm the time,
I feel it more than half a crime
When Nature sleeps and stars are mute,
To mar the silence ev'n with lute.
At rest on ocean's brilliant dyes
An image of Elysium lies:
Seven Pleiades entranced in Heaven,
Form in the deep another seven:
Endymion nodding from above
Sees in the sea a second love:
Within the valleys dim and brown,
And on the spectral mountain's crown,
The wearied light is dying down:
And earth, and stars, and sea, and sky
Are redolent of sleep, as I
Am redolent of thee and thine
Enthralling love, my Adeline.
But list, O list!—so soft and low
Thy lover's voice tonight shall flow
That, scarce awake, thy soul shall deem
My words the music of a dream.
Thus, while no single sound too rude
Upon thy slumber shall intrude,
Our thoughts, our souls—O God above!
In every deed shall mingle, love.

To One in Paradise

Thou wast all that to me, love,
    For which my soul did pine—
A green isle in the sea, love,
    A fountain and a shrine,
All wreathed with fairy fruits and flowers,
    And all the flowers were mine.

Ah, dream too bright to last!
    Ah, starry Hope! that didst arise
But to be overcast!
    A voice from out the Future cries,
"On! on!"—but o'er the Past
    (Dim gulf!) my spirit hovering lies
Mute, motionless, aghast!

For, alas! alas! with me
    The light of Life is o'er!
No more—no more—no more—
    (Such language holds the solemn sea
To the sands upon the shore)
Shall bloom the thunder-blasted tree,
    Or the stricken eagle soar!

And all my days are trances,
    And all my nightly dreams
Are where thy dark eye glances,
    And where thy footstep gleams—
In what ethereal dances,
    By what eternal streams.

The City in the Sea

Lo! Death has reared himself a throne
In a strange city lying alone
Far down within the dim West,
Where the good and the bad and the worst and the best
Have gone to their eternal rest.
There shrines and palaces and towers
(Time-eaten towers that tremble not!)
Resemble nothing that is ours.
Around, by lifting winds forgot,
Resignedly beneath the sky
The melancholy waters lie.

No rays from the holy Heaven come down
On the long night-time of that town;
But light from out the lurid sea
Streams up the turrets silently—
Gleams up the pinnacles far and free—
Up domes—up spires—up kingly halls—
Up fanes—up Babylon-like walls—
Up shadowy long-forgotten bowers
Of sculptured ivy and stone flowers—
Up many and many a marvellous shrine
Whose wreathèd friezes intertwine
The viol, the violet, and the vine.

Resignedly beneath the sky
The melancholy waters lie.
So blend the turrets and shadows there
That all seem pendulous in air,
While from a proud tower in the town

Death looks gigantically down.
There open fanes and gaping graves
Yawn level with the luminous waves;
But not the riches there that lie
In each idol's diamond eye—
Not the gaily-jewelled dead
Tempt the waters from their bed;
For no ripples curl, alas!
Along that wilderness of glass—
No swellings tell that winds may be
Upon some far-off happier sea—
No heavings hint that winds have been
On seas less hideously serene.

But lo, a stir is in the air!
The wave—there is a movement there!
As if the towers had thrown aside,
In slightly sinking, the dull tide—
As if their tops had feebly given
A void within the filmy Heaven.
The waves have now a redder glow—
The hours are breathing faint and low—
And when, amid no earthly moans,
Down, down that town shall settle hence,
Hell, rising from a thousand thrones,
Shall do it reverence.

Israfel

And the angel Israfel, whose
heart-strings are a lute, and
who has the sweetest voice
of all God's creatures.——Koran

In Heaven a spirit doth dwell
    "Whose heart-strings are a lute;"
None sing so wildly well
As the angel Israfel,
And the giddy stars (so legends tell)
Ceasing their hymns, attend the spell
    Of his voice, all mute.

Tottering above
    In her highest noon,
    The enamoured moon
Blushes with love,
    While, to listen, the red levin
    (With the rapid Pleiads, even,
    Which were seven,)
    Pauses in Heaven.

And they say (the starry choir
    And the other listening things)
That Israfeli's fire
Is owing to that lyre
    By which he sits and sings—
The trembling living wire
    Of those unusual strings.

But the skies that angel trod,
    Where deep thoughts are a duty—
Where Love's a grown-up God—
    Where the Houri glances are
Imbued with all the beauty
    Which we worship in a star.

Therefore, thou art not wrong,
    Israfeli, who despisest
An unimpassioned song;
To thee the laurels belong,
    Best bard, because the wisest!
Merrily live, and long!

The ecstasies above
    With thy burning measures suit—
Thy grief, thy joy, thy hate, thy love,
    With the fervour of thy lute—
    Well may the stars be mute!

Yes, Heaven is thine; but this
    Is a world of sweets and sours;
    Our flowers are merely—flowers,
And the shadow of thy perfect bliss
    Is the sunshine of ours.

If I could dwell
Where Israfel
    Hath dwelt, and he where I,
He might not sing so wildly well
    A mortal melody,

While a bolder note than this might swell
  From my lyre within the sky.

Spirits of the Dead

I

Thy soul shall find itself alone
'Mid dark thoughts of the gray tombstone—
Not one, of all the crowd, to pry
Into thine hour of secrecy.

II

Be silent in that solitude,
        Which is not loneliness—for then
The spirits of the dead who stood
        In life before thee are again
In death around thee—and their will
Shall overshadow thee: be still.

III

The night, tho' clear—shall frown—
And the stars shall not look down
From their high thrones in the Heaven,
With light like Hope to mortals given—
But their red orbs, without beam,
To thy weariness shall seem
As a burning and a fever
Which would cling to thee forever.

IV

Now are thoughts thou shalt not banish—
Now are visions ne'er to vanish—
From thy spirit shall they pass
No more—like dew-drops from the grass.

V

The breeze—the breath of God—is still—
And the mist upon the hill
Shadowy—shadowy—yet unbroken,
Is a symbol and a token—
How it hangs upon the trees,
A mystery of mysteries!

A Dream

In visions of the dark night
    I have dreamed of joy departed,
But a waking dream of life and light
    Hath left me broken-hearted.

Ah! what is not a dream by day
    To him whose eyes are cast
On things around him with a ray
    Turned back upon the past?

That holy dream—that holy dream,
    While all the world were chiding,
Hath cheered me as a lovely beam
    A lonely spirit guiding.

What though that light, thro' storm and night,
    So trembled from afar,
What could there be more purely bright
    In Truth's day star?

The Coliseum

Type of the antique Rome! Rich reliquary
Of lofty contemplation left to Time
By buried centuries of pomp and power!
At length—at length—after so many days
Of weary pilgrimage and burning thirst,
(Thirst for the springs of lore that in thee lie),
I kneel, an altered and an humble man,
Amid thy shadows, and so drink within
My very soul thy grandeur, gloom, and glory!

Vastness! and Age! and Memories of Eld!
Silence! and Desolation! and dim Night!
I feel ye now—I feel ye in your strength—
O spells more sure than e'er Judæan king
Taught in the gardens of Gethsemane!
O charms more potent than the rapt Chaldee
Ever drew down from out the quiet stars!

Here, where a hero fell, a column falls!
Here, where the mimic eagle glared in gold,
A midnight vigil holds the swarthy bat!
Here, where the dames of Rome their gilded hair
Waved to the wind, now wave the reed and
    thistle!
Here, where on golden throne the monarch
    lolled,
Glides, spectre-like, unto his marble home,
Lit by the wan light of the hornèd moon,
The swift and silent lizard of the stones!

But stay! these walls—these ivy-clad arcades—
These mouldering plinths—these sad and blackened
    shafts—
These vague entablatures—this crumbling frieze—
These shattered cornices—this wreck—this ruin—
These stones—alas! these gray stones—are they all—
All of the famed, and the colossal left
By the corrosive Hours to Fate and me?

"Not all"—the Echoes answer me—"not all!
Prophetic sounds and loud, arise forever
From us, and from all Ruin, unto the wise,
As melody from Memnon to the Sun.
We rule the hearts of mightiest men—we rule
With a despotic sway all giant minds.
We are not impotent—we pallid stones.
Not all our power is gone—not all our fame—
Not all the magic of our high renown—
Not all the wonder that encircles us—
Not all the mysteries that in us lie—
Not all the memories that hang upon
And cling around about us as a garment,
Clothing us in a robe of more than glory."

The Conqueror Worm

Lo! 'tis a gala night
    Within the lonesome latter years!
An angel throng, bewinged, bedight
    In veils, and drowned in tears,
Sit in a theatre, to see
    A play of hopes and fears,
While the orchestra breathes fitfully
    The music of the spheres.

Mimes, in the form of God on high,
    Mutter and mumble low,
And hither and thither fly—
    Mere puppets they, who come and go
At bidding of vast formless things
    That shift the scenery to and fro,
Flapping from out their Condor wings
    Invisible Woe!

That motley drama—oh, be sure
    It shall not be forgot!
With its Phantom chased for evermore,
    By a crowd that seize it not,
Through a circle that ever returneth in
    To the self-same spot,
And much of Madness, and more of Sin,
    And Horror the soul of the plot.

But see, amid the mimic rout
    A crawling shape intrude!
A blood-red thing that writhes from out

The scenic solitude!
It writhes!—it writhes!—with mortal pangs
    The mimes become its food,
And the angels sob at vermin fangs
    In human gore imbued.

Out—out are the lights—out all!
    And, over each quivering form,
The curtain, a funeral pall,
    Comes down with the rush of a storm,
And the angels, all pallid and wan,
    Uprising, unveiling, affirm
That the play is the tragedy, "Man,"
    And its hero, the Conqueror Worm.

The Haunted Palace

In the greenest of our valleys
  By good angels tenanted,
Once a fair and stately palace—
  Radiant palace—reared its head.
In the monarch Thought's dominion—
  It stood there!
Never seraph spread a pinion
  Over fabric half so fair!

Banners yellow, glorious, golden,
  On its roof did float and flow,
(This—all this—was in the olden
  Time long ago)
And every gentle air that dallied,
  In that sweet day,
Along the ramparts plumed and pallid,
  A wingèd odor went away.

Wanderers in that happy valley,
  Through two luminous windows, saw
Spirits moving musically,
  To a lute's well-tunèd law,
Round about a throne, where sitting,
  Porphyrogene!
In state his glory well befitting,
  The ruler of the realm was seen.

And all with pearl and ruby glowing
  Was the fair palace door,
Through which came flowing, flowing, flowing,

And sparkling evermore,
A troop of Echoes, whose sweet duty
    Was but to sing,
In voices of surpassing beauty,
    The wit and wisdom of their king.

But evil things, in robes of sorrow,
    Assailed the monarch's high estate.
(Ah, let us mourn!—for never morrow
    Shall dawn upon him desolate!)
And round about his home the glory
    That blushed and bloomed,
Is but a dim-remembered story
    Of the old time entombed.

And travellers, now, within that valley,
    Through the red-litten windows see
Vast forms that move fantastically
    To a discordant melody,
While, like a ghastly rapid river,
    Through the pale door
A hideous throng rush out forever
    And laugh—but smile no more.

Al Aaraf

PART I

O! Nothing earthly save the ray
(Thrown back from flowers) of Beauty's eye,
As in those gardens where the day
Springs from the gems of Circassy—
O! nothing earthly save the thrill
Of melody in woodland rill—
Or (music of the passion-hearted)
Joy's voice so peacefully departed
That, like the murmur in the shell,
Its echo dwelleth and will dwell—
Oh, nothing of the dross of ours—
Yet all the beauty—all the flowers
That, list our Love, and deck our bowers—
Adorn yon world afar, afar—
The wandering star.

'Twas a sweet time for Nesace—for there
Her world lay lolling on the golden air,
Near four bright suns—a temporary rest—
An oasis in desert of the blest.
Away—away—'mid seas of rays that roll
Empyrean splendor o'er th' unchained soul—
The soul that scarce (the billows are so dense)
Can struggle to its destin'd eminence—
To distant spheres, from time to time, she rode,
And late to ours, the favor'd one of God—
But, now, the ruler of an anchor'd realm,
She throws aside the sceptre—leaves the helm,

And, amid incense and high spiritual hymns,
Laves in quadruple light her angel limbs.

Now happiest, loveliest in yon lovely Earth,
Whence sprang the "Idea of Beauty" into birth,
(Falling in wreaths thro' many a startled star,
Like woman's hair 'mid pearls, until, afar,
It lit on hills Achaian, and there dwelt),
She look'd into Infinity—and knelt.
Rich clouds, for canopies, about her curled—
Fit emblems of the model of her world—
Seen but in beauty—not impeding sight—
Of other beauty glittering thro' the light—
A wreath that twined each starry form around,
And all the opal'd air in color bound.

All hurriedly she knelt upon a bed
Of flowers: of lilies such as rear'd the head
On the fair Capo Deucato, and sprang
So eagerly around about to hang
Upon the flying footsteps of—deep pride—
Of her who lov'd a mortal—and so died.
The Sephalica, budding with young bees,
Uprear'd its purple stem around her knees:
And gemmy flower, of Trebizond misnam'd—
Inmate of highest stars, where erst it sham'd
All other loveliness: its honied dew
(The fabled nectar that the heathen knew)
Deliriously sweet, was dropp'd from Heaven,
And fell on gardens of the unforgiven
In Trebizond—and on a sunny flower
So like its own above, that to this hour,

It still remaineth, torturing the bee
With madness, and unwonted reverie:
In Heaven, and all its environs, the leaf
And blossom of the fairy plant, in grief
Disconsolate linger—grief that hangs her head,
Repenting follies that full long have fled,
Heaving her white breast to the balmy air,
Like guilty beauty, chasten'd, and more fair:
Nyctanthes too, as sacred as the light
She fears to perfume, perfuming the night:
And Clytia pondering between many a sun,
While pettish tears adown her petals run:
And that aspiring flower that sprang on Earth—
And died, ere scarce exalted into birth,
Bursting its odorous heart in spirit to wing
Its way to Heaven, from garden of a king:
And Valisnerian lotus thither flown
From struggling with the waters of the Rhone:
And thy most lovely purple perfume, Zante!
Isola d'oro!—Fior di Levante!
And the Nelumbo bud that floats for ever
With Indian Cupid down the holy river—
Fair flowers, and fairy! to whose care is given
To bear the Goddess' song, in odors, up to Heaven:

"Spirit! that dwellest where,
        In the deep sky,
The terrible and fair,
        In beauty vie!
Beyond the line of blue—
        The boundary of the star
Which turneth at the view

Of thy barrier and thy bar—
Of the barrier overgone
        By the comets who were cast
From their pride, and from their throne
        To be drudges till the last—
To be carriers of fire
        (The red fire of their heart)
With speed that may not tire
        And with pain that shall not part—
Who livest—*that* we know—
        In Eternity—we feel—
But the shadow of whose brow
        What spirit shall reveal?
Tho' the beings whom thy Nesace,
        Thy messenger, hath known,
Have dream'd for thy Infinity
        A model of their own—
Thy will is done, O God!
        The star hath ridden high
Thro' many a tempest, but she rode
        Beneath thy burning eye;
And here, in thought, to thee—
        In thought that can alone
Ascend thy empire and so be
        A partner of thy throne—
By winged Fantasy,
        My embassy is given,
Till secrecy shall knowledge be
        In the environs of Heaven."

She ceas'd—and buried then her burning cheek
Abash'd, amid the lilies there, to seek

A shelter from the fervour of His eye;
For the stars trembled at the Deity.
She stirr'd not—breath'd not—for a voice was there
How solemnly pervading the calm air!
A sound of silence on the startled ear
Which dreamy poets name "the music of the
    sphere."
Ours is a world of words: Quiet we call
"Silence"—which is the merest word of all.
All Nature speaks, and ev'n ideal things
Flap shadowy sounds from the visionary wings—
But ah! not so when, thus, in realms on high
The eternal voice of God is passing by,
And the red winds are withering in the sky!
"What tho' in worlds which sightless cycles run,
Link'd to a little system, and one sun—
Where all my love is folly, and the crowd
Still think my terrors but the thunder cloud,
The storm, the earthquake, and the ocean-wrath—
(Ah! will they cross me in my angrier path?)
What tho' in worlds which own a single sun
The sands of Time grow dimmer as they run,
Yet thine is my resplendency, so given
To bear my secrets thro' the upper Heaven.
Leave tenantless thy crystal home, and fly,
With all thy train, athwart the moony sky—
Apart—like fire-flies in Sicilian night,
And wing to other worlds another light!
Divulge the secrets of thy embassy
To the proud orbs that twinkle—and so be
To ev'ry heart a barrier and a ban
Lest the stars totter in the guilt of man!"

Up rose the maiden in the yellow night,
The single-mooned eve!—on Earth we plight
Our faith to one love—and one moon adore—
The birth-place of young Beauty had no more.
As sprang that yellow star from downy hours,
Up rose the maiden from her shrine of flowers,
And bent o'er sheeny mountain and dim plain
Her way—but left not yet her Therasæan reign.

PART II

High on a mountain of enamell'd head—
Such as the drowsy shepherd on his bed
Of giant pasturage lying at his ease,
Raising his heavy eyelid, starts and sees
With many a mutter'd "hope to be forgiven"
What time the moon is quadrated in Heaven—
Of rosy head, that towering far away
Into the sunlit ether, caught the ray
Of sunken suns at eve—at noon of night,
While the moon danc'd with the fair stranger light—
Uprear'd upon such height arose a pile
Of gorgeous columns on th' unburthen'd air,
Flashing from Parian marble that twin smile
Far down upon the wave that sparkled there,
And nursled the young mountain in its lair.
Of molten stars their pavement, such as fall
Thro' the ebon air, besilvering the pall
Of their own dissolution, while they die—
Adorning then the dwellings of the sky.
A dome, by linked light from Heaven let down,
Sat gently on these columns as a crown—

A window of one circular diamond, there,
Look'd out above into the purple air
And rays from God shot down that meteor chain
And hallow'd all the beauty twice again,
Save when, between th' Empyrean and that ring,
Some eager spirit flapp'd his dusky wing.
But on the pillars Seraph eyes have seen
The dimness of this world: that grayish green
That Nature loves the best for Beauty's grave
Lurk'd in each cornice, round each architrave—
And every sculptur'd cherub thereabout
That from his marble dwelling peerèd out,
Seem'd earthly in the shadow of his niche—
Achaian statues in a world so rich?
Friezes from Tadmor and Persepolis—
From Balbec, and the stilly, clear abyss
Of beautiful Gomorrah! Oh, the wave
Is now upon thee—but too late to save!

Sound loves to revel in a summer night:
Witness the murmur of the gray twilight
That stole upon the ear, in Eyraco,
Of many a wild star-gazer long ago—
That stealeth ever on the ear of him
Who, musing, gazeth on the distance dim,
And sees the darkness coming as a cloud—
Is not its form—its voice—most palpable and loud?

But what is this?—it cometh—and it brings
A music with it—'tis the rush of wings—
A pause—and then a sweeping, falling strain,
And Nesace is in her halls again.

From the wild energy of wanton haste
      Her cheeks were flushing, and her lips apart;
The zone that clung around her gentle waist
      Had burst beneath the heaving of her heart.
Within the centre of that hall to breathe
She paus'd and panted, Zanthe! all beneath,
The fairy light that kiss'd her golden hair
And long'd to rest, yet could but sparkle there!

Young flowers were whispering in melody
To happy flowers that night—and tree to tree;
Fountains were gushing music as they fell
In many a star-lit grove, or moon-light dell;
Yet silence came upon material things—
Fair flowers, bright waterfalls and angel wings—
And sound alone that from the spirit sprang
Bore burthen to the charm the maiden sang:

"'Neath blue-bell or streamer—
      Or tufted wild spray
That keeps from the dreamer
      The moonbeam away—
Bright beings! that ponder,
      With half closing eyes,
On the stars which your wonder
      Hath drawn from the skies,
Till they glance thro' the shade, and
      Come down to your brow
Like—eyes of the maiden
      Who calls on you now—
Arise! from your dreaming
      In violet bowers,

To duty beseeming
        These star-litten hours—
And shake from your tresses,
        Encumber'd with dew,
The breath of those kisses
        That cumber them too—
(O! how, without you, Love!
        Could angels be blest?)—
Those kisses of true love
        That lull'd ye to rest!
Up!—shake from your wing
        Each hindering thing:
The dew of the night—
        It would weigh down your flight;
And true love caresses—
        O! leave them apart!
They are light on the tresses,
        But lead on the heart.

"Ligeia! Ligeia!
        My beautiful one!
Whose harshest idea
        Will to melody run,
O! is it thy will
        On the breezes to toss?
Or, capriciously still,
        Like the lone Albatross,
Incumbent on night
        (As she on the air)
To keep watch with delight
        On the harmony there?

"Ligeia! wherever
        Thy image may be,
No magic shall sever
        Thy music from thee.
Thou hast bound many eyes
        In a dreamy sleep—
But the strains still arise
        Which thy vigilance keep:
The sound of the rain
        Which leaps down to the flower,
And dances again
        In the rhythm of the shower—
The murmur that springs
        From the growing of grass
Are the music of things—
        But are modell'd, alas!—
Away, then, my dearest,
        O! hie thee away
To springs that lie clearest
        Beneath the moon-ray—
To lone lake that smiles,
        In its dream of deep rest,
At the many star-isles
        That enjewel its breast—
Where wild flowers, creeping,
        Have mingled their shade,
On its margin is sleeping
        Full many a maid—
Some have left the cool glade, and
        Have slept with the bee—
Arouse them, my maiden,
        On moorland and lea—

Go! breathe on their slumber,
    All softly in ear,
The musical number
    They slumber'd to hear—
For what can awaken
    An angel so soon
Whose sleep hath been taken
    Beneath the cold moon,
As the spell which no slumber
    Of witchery may test,
The rhythmical number
    Which lull'd him to rest?"

Spirits in wing, and angels to the view,
A thousand seraphs burst th' Empyrean thro',
Young dreams still hovering on their drowsy flight—
Seraphs in all but "Knowledge," the keen light
That fell, refracted, thro' thy bounds afar,
O death! from eye of God upon that star:
Sweet was that error—sweeter still that death—
Sweet was that error—ev'n with us the breath
Of Science dims the mirror of our joy—
To them 'twere the Simoom, and would destroy—
For what (to them) availeth it to know
That Truth is Falsehood—or that Bliss is Woe?
Sweet was their death—with them to die was rife
With the last ecstasy of satiate life—
Beyond that death no immortality—
But sleep that pondereth and is not "to be"—
And there—oh! may my weary spirit dwell—
Apart from Heaven's Eternity—and yet how far from Hell!

What guilty spirit, in what shrubbery dim
Heard not the stirring summons of that hymn?
But two: they fell: for Heaven no grace imparts
To those who hear not for their beating hearts.
A maiden-angel and her seraph-lover—
O! where (and ye may seek the wide skies over)
Was Love, the blind, near sober Duty known?
Unguided Love hath fallen—'mid "tears of perfect
    moan."

He was a goodly spirit—he who fell:
A wanderer by mossy-mantled well—
A gazer on the lights that shine above—
A dreamer in the moonbeam by his love:
What wonder? for each star is eye-like there,
And looks so sweetly down on Beauty's hair;
And they, and ev'ry mossy spring were holy
To his love-haunted heart and melancholy.
The night had found (to him a night of woe)
Upon a mountain crag, young Angelo—
Beetling it bends athwart the solemn sky,
And scowls on starry worlds that down beneath it lie.
Here sate he with his love—his dark eye bent
With eagle gaze along the firmament:
Now turn'd it upon her—but ever then
It trembled to the orb of EARTH again.

"Ianthe, dearest, see! how dim that ray!
How lovely 'tis to look so far away!
She seem'd not thus upon that autumn eve
I left her gorgeous halls—nor mourn'd to leave,
That eve—that eve—I should remember well—

The sun-ray dropp'd in Lemnos, with a spell
On th' Arabesque carving of a gilded hall
Wherein I sate, and on the draperied wall—
And on my eyelids—O, the heavy light!
How drowsily it weighed them into night!
On flowers, before, and mist, and love they ran
With Persian Saadi in his Gulistan:
But O, that light!—I slumber'd—Death, the while,
Stole o'er my senses in that lovely isle
So softly that no single silken hair
Awoke that slept—or knew that he was there.

"The last spot of Earth's orb I trod upon
Was a proud temple call'd the Parthenon;
More beauty clung around her column'd wall
Then ev'n thy glowing bosom beats withal,
And when old Time my wing did disenthral—
Thence sprang I—as the eagle from his tower,
And years I left behind me in an hour.
What time upon her airy bounds I hung,
One half the garden of her globe was flung
Unrolling as a chart unto my view—
Tenantless cities of the desert too!
Ianthe, beauty crowded on me then,
And half I wish'd to be again of men."

"My Angelo! and why of them to be?
A brighter dwelling-place is here for thee—
And greener fields than in yon world above,
And woman's loveliness—and passionate love."

"But list, Ianthe! when the air so soft
Fail'd, as my pennon'd spirit leapt aloft,
Perhaps my brain grew dizzy—but the world
I left so late was into chaos hurl'd—
Sprang from her station, on the winds apart,
And roll'd, a flame, the fiery Heaven athwart.
Methought, my sweet one, then I ceased to soar,
And fell—not swiftly as I rose before,
But with a downward, tremulous motion thro'
Light, brazen rays, this golden star unto!
Nor long the measure of my falling hours,
For nearest of all stars was thine to ours—
Dread star! that came, amid a night of mirth,
A red Dædalion on the timid Earth."

"We came—and to thy Earth—but not to us
Be given our lady's bidding to discuss:
We came, my love; around, above, below,
Gay fire-fly of the night we come and go,
Nor ask a reason save the angel-nod
She grants to us as granted by her God—
But, Angelo, than thine gray Time unfurl'd
Never his fairy wing o'er fairer world!
Dim was its little disk, and angel eyes
Alone could see the phantom in the skies,
When first Al Aaraaf knew her course to be
Headlong thitherward o'er the starry sea—
But when its glory swell'd upon the sky,
As glowing Beauty's bust beneath man's eye,
We paus'd before the heritage of men,
And thy star trembled—as doth Beauty then!"

Thus in discourse, the lovers whiled away
The night that waned and waned and brought no day.
They fell: for Heaven to them no hope imparts
Who hear not for the beating of their hearts.

Sonnet—Silence

There are some qualities—some incorporate things,
    That have a double life, which thus is made
A type of that twin entity which springs
    From matter and light, evinced in solid and shade.
There is a two-fold *Silence*—sea and shore—
    Body and soul. One dwells in lonely places,
    Newly with grass o'ergrown; some solemn graces,
Some human memories and tearful lore,
Render him terrorless: his name's "No More."
He is the corporate Silence: dread him not!
    No power hath he of evil in himself;
But should some urgent fate (untimely lot!)
    Bring thee to meet his shadow (nameless elf,
That haunteth the lone regions where hath trod
No foot of man), commend thyself to God!

Dream-Land

By a route obscure and lonely,
Haunted by ill angels only,
Where an Eidolon, named NIGHT,
On a black throne reigns upright,
I have reached these lands but newly
From an ultimate dim Thule—
From a wild weird clime that lieth, sublime,
    Out of SPACE—out of TIME.

Bottomless vales and boundless floods,
And chasms, and caves, and Titan woods,
With forms that no man can discover
For the dews that drip all over;
Mountains toppling evermore
Into seas without a shore;
Seas that restlessly aspire,
Surging, unto skies of fire;
Lakes that endlessly outspread
Their lone waters—lone and dead,—
Their still waters—still and chilly
With the snows of the lolling lily.

By the lakes that thus outspread
Their lone waters, lone and dead,—
Their sad waters, sad and chilly
With the snows of the lolling lily,—
By the mountains—near the river
Murmuring lowly, murmuring ever,—
By the gray woods,—by the swamp
Where the toad and the newt encamp,—

By the dismal tarns and pools
        Where dwell the Ghouls,—
By each spot the most unholy—
In each nook most melancholy,—
There the traveller meets, aghast,
Sheeted Memories of the Past—
Shrouded forms that start and sigh
As they pass the wanderer by—
White-robed forms of friends long given,
In agony, to the Earth—and Heaven.

For the heart whose woes are legion
'Tis a peaceful, soothing region—
For the spirit that walks in shadow
'Tis—oh 'tis an Eldorado!
But the traveller, travelling through it,
May not—dare not openly view it;
Never its mysteries are exposed
To the weak human eye unclosed;
So wills its King, who hath forbid
The uplifting of the fringèd lid;
And thus the sad Soul that here passes
Beholds it but through darkened glasses.

By a route obscure and lonely,
Haunted by ill angels only,
Where an Eidolon, named NIGHT,
On a black throne reigns upright,
I have wandered home but newly
From this ultimate dim Thule.

The Raven

Once upon a midnight dreary, while I pondered, weak
and weary,
Over many a quaint and curious volume of forgotten
lore—
While I nodded, nearly napping, suddenly there came a
tapping,
As of some one gently rapping, rapping at my chamber
door.
"'Tis some visitor," I muttered, "tapping at my chamber
door—
                    Only this and nothing more."

Ah, distinctly I remember it was in the bleak
December;
And each separate dying ember wrought its ghost upon
the floor.
Eagerly I wished the morrow;—vainly I had sought to
borrow
From my books surcease of sorrow—sorrow for the lost
Lenore—
For the rare and radiant maiden whom the angels name
Lenore—
                    Nameless here for evermore.

And the silken, sad, uncertain rustling of each purple
curtain
Thrilled me—filled me with fantastic terrors never felt
before;
So that now, to still the beating of my heart, I stood
repeating,

"'Tis some visitor entreating entrance at my chamber
   door—
Some late visitor entreating entrance at my chamber
   door;—
                     This it is, and nothing more."

Presently my soul grew stronger; hesitating then no
   longer,
"Sir," said I, "or Madam, truly your forgiveness I
   implore;
But the fact is I was napping, and so gently you came
   rapping,
And so faintly you came tapping, tapping at my chamber
   door,
That I scarce was sure I heard you"—here I opened wide
   the
door;—
                     Darkness there and nothing more.

Deep into that darkness peering, long I stood there
   wondering, fearing,
Doubting, dreaming dreams no mortal ever dared to
   dream before;
But the silence was unbroken, and the stillness gave no
   token,
And the only word there spoken was the whispered word,
   "Lenore?"
This I whispered, and an echo murmured back the word,
   "Lenore!"
                     Merely this and nothing more.

Back into the chamber turning, all my soul within me
  burning,
Soon again I heard a tapping somewhat louder than
  before.
"Surely," said I, "surely that is something at my window
  lattice;
Let me see, then, what thereat is, and this mystery
  explore—
Let my heart be still a moment and this mystery
  explore;—
     'Tis the wind and nothing more!"

Open here I flung the shutter, when, with many a flirt
  and flutter,
In there stepped a stately Raven of the saintly days of
  yore;
Not the least obeisance made he; not a minute stopped or
  stayed he;
But, with mien of lord or lady, perched above my
  chamber door—
Perched upon a bust of Pallas just above my chamber
  door—
    Perched, and sat, and nothing more.

Then this ebony bird beguiling my sad fancy into
  smiling,
By the grave and stern decorum of the countenance it
  wore,
"Though thy crest be shorn and shaven, thou," I said, "art
  sure no craven,

Ghastly grim and ancient Raven wandering from the Nightly
    shore—
Tell me what thy lordly name is on the Night's Plutonian
    shore!"
                         Quoth the Raven, "Nevermore."

Much I marvelled this ungainly fowl to hear discourse so
    plainly,
Though its answer little meaning—little relevancy
    bore;
For we cannot help agreeing that no living human being
Ever yet was blessed with seeing bird above his chamber
    door—
Bird or beast upon the sculptured bust above his chamber
    door,
                         With such name as "Nevermore."

But the Raven, sitting lonely on the placid bust, spoke
    only
That one word, as if his soul in that one word he did
    outpour.
Nothing farther then he uttered—not a feather then he
    fluttered—
Till I scarcely more than muttered, "Other friends have flown
    before—
On the morrow *he* will leave me, as my Hopes have flown
    before."
                         Then the bird said, "Nevermore."

Startled at the stillness broken by reply so aptly spoken,
"Doubtless," said I, "what it utters is its only stock and
    store

Caught from some unhappy master whom unmerciful
    Disaster
Followed fast and followed faster till his songs one burden
    bore—
Till the dirges of his Hope that melancholy burden bore
                    Of 'Never—nevermore.'"

But the Raven still beguiling all my sad soul into smiling,
Straight I wheeled a cushioned seat in front of bird, and
    bust and door;
Then, upon the velvet sinking, I betook myself to linking
Fancy unto fancy, thinking what this ominous bird of
    yore—
What this grim, ungainly, ghastly, gaunt and ominous bird
    of yore
                    Meant in croaking "Nevermore."

This I sat engaged in guessing, but no syllable
    expressing
To the fowl whose fiery eyes now burned into my
    bosom's core;
This and more I sat divining, with my head at ease
    reclining
On the cushion's velvet lining that the lamp-light gloated
    o'er,
But whose velvet violet lining with the lamp-light
    gloating o'er,
        She shall press, ah, nevermore!

Then, methought, the air grew denser, perfumed from an
    unseen censer

Swung by Seraphim whose faint foot-falls tinkled on the
tufted floor.
"Wretch," I cried, "thy God hath lent thee—by these
angels he hath sent thee
Respite—respite and nepenthe from thy memories of Lenore!
Quaff, oh quaff this kind nepenthe and forget this lost
Lenore!"

      Quoth the Raven, "Nevermore."

"Prophet!" said I, "thing of evil!—prophet still, if bird or
devil!—
Whether Tempter sent, or whether tempest tossed thee
here ashore,
Desolate yet all undaunted, on this desert land
enchanted—
On this home by Horror haunted—tell me truly, I
implore—
Is there—is there balm in Gilead?—tell me—tell me, I
implore!"

      Quoth the Raven, "Nevermore."

"Prophet!" said I, "thing of evil!—prophet still, if bird or
devil!
By that Heaven that bends above us—by that God we
both adore—
Tell this soul with sorrow laden if, within the distant
Aidenn,
It shall clasp a sainted maiden whom the angels name
Lenore—
Clasp a rare and radiant maiden whom the angels name
Lenore."

      Quoth the Raven, "Nevermore."

"Be that word our sign of parting, bird or fiend!" I
    shrieked, upstarting—
"Get thee back into the tempest and the Night's Plutonian
    shore!
Leave no black plume as a token of that lie thy soul hath
    spoken!
Leave my loneliness unbroken!—quit the bust above my
    door!
Take thy beak from out my heart, and take thy form from
    off my door!"
                    Quoth the Raven, "Nevermore."

And the Raven, never flitting, still is sitting, still is sitting
On the pallid bust of Pallas just above my chamber door;
And his eyes have all the seeming of a demon's that is
    dreaming,
And the lamp-light o'er him streaming throws his shadow
    on the floor;
And my soul from out that shadow that lies floating on
    the floor
                    Shall be lifted—nevermore!

The Sleeper

At midnight, in the month of June,
I stand beneath the mystic moon.
An opiate vapour, dewy, dim,
Exhales from out her golden rim,
And, softly dripping, drop by drop,
Upon the quiet mountain top,
Steals drowsily and musically
Into the universal valley.
The rosemary nods upon the grave;
The lily lolls upon the wave;
Wrapping the fog about its breast,
The ruin moulders into rest;
Looking like Lethe, see! the lake
A conscious slumber seems to take,
And would not, for the world, awake.
All Beauty sleeps!—and lo! where lies
Irene, with her Destinies!

Oh, lady bright! can it be right—
This window open to the night!
The wanton airs, from the tree-top,
Laughingly through the lattice-drop—
The bodiless airs, a wizard rout,
Flit through thy chamber in and out,
And wave the curtain canopy
So fitfully—so fearfully—
Above the closed and fringèd lid
'Neath which thy slumb'ring soul lies hid,
That, o'er the floor and down the wall,
Like ghosts the shadows rise and fall!

Oh, lady dear, hast thou no fear?
Why and what art thou dreaming here?
Sure thou art come o'er far-off seas,
A wonder to these garden trees!
Strange is thy pallor! strange thy dress!
Strange, above all, thy length of tress,
And this all-solemn silentness!

The lady sleeps! Oh, may her sleep
Which is enduring, so be deep!
Heaven have her in its sacred keep!
This chamber changed for one more holy,
This bed for one more melancholy,
I pray to God that she may lie
Forever with unopened eye,
While the pale sheeted ghosts go by!

My love, she sleeps! Oh, may her sleep,
As it is lasting, so be deep;
Soft may the worms about her creep!
Far in the forest, dim and old,
For her may some tall vault unfold—
Some vault that oft hath flung its black
And wingèd panels fluttering back,
Triumphant, o'er the crested palls,
Of her grand family funerals—

Some sepulchre, remote, alone,
Against whose portal she hath thrown,
In childhood many an idle stone—
Some tomb from out whose sounding door
She ne'er shall force an echo more,

Thrilling to think, poor child of sin!
It was the dead who groaned within.

The Divine Right of Kings

The only king by right divine
Is Ellen King, and were she mine
I'd strive for liberty no more,
But hug the glorious chains I wore.

Her bosom is an ivory throne,
Where tyrant virtue reigns alone;
No subject vice dare interfere,
To check the power that governs here.

O! would she deign to rule my fate,
I'd worship Kings and kingly state,
And hold this maxim all life long,
The King—my King—can do no wrong.

Impromptu. To Kate Carol

When from your gems of thought I turn
To those pure orbs, your heart to learn,
I scarce know which to prize most high—
The bright i-*dea*, or the bright *dear-eye*.

An Epigram for Wall Street

I'll tell you a plan for gaining wealth,
    Better than banking, trade or leases—
Take a bank note and fold it up,
    And then you will find your money in creases!
This wonderful plan, without danger or loss,
      Keeps your cash in your hands, where nothing
        can trouble it;
And every time that you fold it across,
      'Tis as plain as the light of the day that you double
        it!

To F——

Beloved! amid the earnest woes
  That crowd around my earthly path—
(Drear path, alas! where grows
Not even one lonely rose)—
  My soul at least a solace hath
In dreams of thee, and therein knows
An Eden of bland repose.

And thus thy memory is to me
  Like some enchanted far-off isle
In some tumultuous sea—
Some ocean throbbing far and free
  With storm—but where meanwhile
Serenest skies continually
Just o'er that one bright inland smile.

To F———s S. O———d

Thou wouldst be loved?—then let thy heart
    From its present pathway part not;
Being everything which now thou art,
    Be nothing which thou art not.
So with the world thy gentle ways,
    Thy grace, thy more than beauty,
Shall be an endless theme of praise.
And love a simple duty.

Eulalie—A Song

I dwelt alone
In a world of moan,
And my soul was a stagnant tide,
Till the fair and gentle Eulalie became my blushing
bride—
Till the yellow-haired young Eulalie became my smiling
bride.

Ah, less—less bright
The stars of the night
Than the eyes of the radiant girl!
And never a flake
That the vapor can make
With the moon-tints of purple and pearl,
Can vie with the modest Eulalie's most unregarded curl—
Can compare with the bright-eyed Eulalie's most humble
and careless curl.

Now Doubt—now Pain
Come never again,
For her soul gives me sigh for sigh,
And all day long
Shines, bright and strong,
Astarte within the sky,
While ever to her dear Eulalie upturns her matron eye—
While ever to her young Eulalie upturns her violet eye.

To Helen

I saw thee once—once only—years ago:
I must not say how many—but not many.
It was a July midnight; and from out
A full-orbed moon, that, like thine own soul, soaring,
Sought a precipitate pathway up through heaven,
There fell a silvery-silken veil of light,
With quietude, and sultriness, and slumber,
Upon the upturn'd faces of a thousand
Roses that grew in an enchanted garden,
Where no wind dared to stir, unless on tiptoe—
Fell on the upturn'd faces of these roses
That gave out, in return for the love-light,
Their odorous souls in an ecstatic death—
Fell on the upturn'd faces of these roses
That smiled and died in this parterre, enchanted
By thee, and by the poetry of thy presence.

Clad all in white, upon a violet bank
I saw thee half reclining; while the moon
Fell on the upturn'd faces of the roses,
And on thine own, upturn'd—alas, in sorrow!

Was it not Fate, that, on this July midnight—
Was it not Fate (whose name is also Sorrow),
That bade me pause before that garden-gate,
To breathe the incense of those slumbering roses?
No footstep stirred: the hated world all slept,
Save only thee and me. (O Heaven!—O God!
How my heart beats in coupling those two words!
Save only thee and me.) I paused—I looked—

And in an instant all things disappeared.
(Ah, bear in mind this garden was enchanted!)
The pearly lustre of the moon went out:
The mossy banks and the meandering paths,
The happy flowers and the repining trees,
Were seen no more: the very roses' odors
Died in the arms of the adoring airs.
All—all expired save thee—save less than thou:
Save only the divine light in thine eyes—
Save but the soul in thine uplifted eyes.
I saw but them—they were the world to me.
I saw but them—saw only them for hours—
Saw only them until the moon went down.
What wild heart-histories seemed to lie unwritten
Upon those crystalline, celestial spheres!
How dark a woe! yet how sublime a hope!
How silently serene a sea of pride!
How daring an ambition! yet how deep—
How fathomless a capacity for love!

But now, at length, dear Dian sank from sight,
Into a western couch of thunder-cloud;
And thou, a ghost, amid the entombing trees
Didst glide away. *Only thine eyes remained.*
They *would not* go—they never yet have gone.
Lighting my lonely pathway home that night,
They have not left me (as my hopes have) since.
They follow me—they lead me through the years.
They are my ministers—yet I their slave.
Their office is to illumine and enkindle—
My duty, *to be saved* by their bright light,
And purified in their electric fire,

And sanctified in their elysian fire.
They fill my soul with Beauty (which is Hope),
And are far up in Heaven—the stars I kneel to
In the sad, silent watches of my night;
While even in the meridian glare of day
I see them still—two sweetly scintillant
Venuses, unextinguished by the sun!

Beloved Physician (unfinished)

The pulse beats ten and intermits;
God nerve the soul that ne'er forgets
In calm or storm, by night or day,
Its steady toil, its loyalty.

The pulse beats ten and intermits;
God shield the soul that ne'er forgets.

The pulse beats ten and intermits;
God guide the soul that ne'er forgets.

[. . .] so tired, so weary,
The soft head bows, the sweet eyes close,
The faithful heart yields to repose.

An Enigma

"Seldom we find," says Solomon Don Dunce,
    "Half an idea in the profoundest sonnet.
Through all the flimsy things we see at once
    As easily as through a Naples bonnet—
    Trash of all trash!—how *can* a lady don it?
Yet heavier far than your Petrarchan stuff—
Owl-downy nonsense that the faintest puff
    Twirls into trunk-paper the while you con it."
And, veritably, Sol is right enough.
The general tuckermanities are arrant
Bubbles—ephemeral and *so* transparent—
But *this is*, now—you may depend upon it—
Stable, opaque, immortal—all by dint
Of the dear names that lie concealed within't.

Ulalume—A Ballad

The skies they were ashen and sober;
  The leaves they were crispèd and sere—
  The leaves they were withering and sere:
It was night in the lonesome October
  Of my most immemorial year:
It was hard by the dim lake of Auber,
  In the misty mid region of Weir—
It was down by the dank tarn of Auber,
  In the ghoul-haunted woodland of Weir.

Here once, through an alley Titanic.
  Of cypress, I roamed with my Soul—
  Of cypress, with Psyche, my Soul.
These were days when my heart was volcanic
  As the scoriac rivers that roll—
  As the lavas that restlessly roll
Their sulphurous currents down Yaanek
  In the ultimate climes of the pole—
That groan as they roll down Mount Yaanek
  In the realms of the boreal pole.

Our talk had been serious and sober,
  But our thoughts they were palsied and sere—
  Our memories were treacherous and sere—
For we knew not the month was October,
  And we marked not the night of the year—
  (Ah, night of all nights in the year!)
We noted not the dim lake of Auber—
  (Though once we had journeyed down here)—

We remembered not the dank tarn of Auber,
    Nor the ghoul-haunted woodland of Weir.

And now, as the night was senescent
    And star-dials pointed to morn—
    As the sun-dials hinted of morn—
At the end of our path a liquescent
    And nebulous lustre was born,
Out of which a miraculous crescent
    Arose with a duplicate horn—
Astarte's bediamonded crescent
    Distinct with its duplicate horn.

And I said: "She is warmer than Dian;
    She rolls through an ether of sighs—
    She revels in a region of sighs.
She has seen that the tears are not dry on
    These cheeks, where the worm never dies,
And has come past the stars of the Lion
    To point us the path to the skies—
    To the Lethean peace of the skies—
Come up, in despite of the Lion,
    To shine on us with her bright eyes—
Come up through the lair of the Lion,
    With love in her luminous eyes."

But Psyche, uplifting her finger,
    Said: "Sadly this star I mistrust—
    Her pallor I strangely mistrust:
Ah, hasten!—ah, let us not linger!
    Ah, fly!—let us fly!—for we must."
In terror she spoke, letting sink her

Wings till they trailed in the dust—
In agony sobbed, letting sink her
Plumes till they trailed in the dust—
Till they sorrowfully trailed in the dust.

I replied: "This is nothing but dreaming:
Let us on by this tremulous light!
Let us bathe in this crystalline light!
Its Sibyllic splendor is beaming
With Hope and in Beauty to-night:—
See!—it flickers up the sky through the night!
Ah, we safely may trust to its gleaming,
And be sure it will lead us aright—
We safely may trust to a gleaming
That cannot but guide us aright,
Since it flickers up to Heaven through the night."

Thus I pacified Psyche and kissed her,
And tempted her out of her gloom—
And conquered her scruples and gloom;
And we passed to the end of a vista,
But were stopped by the door of a tomb—
By the door of a legended tomb;
And I said—"What is written, sweet sister,
On the door of this legended tomb?"
She replied—"Ulalume—Ulalume—
'Tis the vault of thy lost Ulalume!"

Then my heart it grew ashen and sober
As the leaves that were crispèd and sere—
As the leaves that were withering and sere;
And I cried: "It was surely October

On this very night of last year
        That I journeyed—I journeyed down here!—
        That I brought a dread burden down here—
        On this night of all nights in the year,
        Ah, what demon has tempted me here?
Well I know, now, this dim lake of Auber—
        This misty mid region of Weir—
Well I know, now, this dank tarn of Auber,
        This ghoul-haunted woodland of Weir."

Said we, then,—the two, then: "Ah can it
        Have been that the woodlandish ghouls—
        The pitiful, the merciful ghouls—
To bar up our way and to ban it
        From the secret that lies in these wolds—
        From the thing that lies hidden in these worlds—
Have drawn up the spectre of a planet
        From the limbo of lunary souls—
This sinfully scintillant planet
        From the Hell of the planetary souls?"

To M. L. S——

Of all who hail thy presence as the morning—
Of all to whom thine absence is the night—
The blotting utterly from out high heaven
The sacred sun—of all who, weeping, bless thee
Hourly for hope—for life—ah! above all,
For the resurrection of deep buried faith
In Truth, in Virtue, in Humanity—
Of all who, on Despair's unhallowed bed
Lying down to die, have suddenly arisen
At thy soft-murmured words, "Let there be light!"
At thy soft-murmured words that were fulfilled
In thy seraphic glancing of thine eyes—
Of all who owe thee most—whose gratitude
Nearest resembles worship,—oh, remember
The truest—the most fervently devoted,
And think that these weak lines are written by him—
By him who, as he pens them, thrills to think
His spirit is communing with an angel's.

Evangeline

Do tell when shall we make common sense men out of
    the owl-eyed pundits
Out of The Frog-faced stupid old God-born Pundits who
    lost in a fog-bank
Strut about all along shore there somewhere close by the
    Down East
Frog Duck Pond munching of pea nuts and pumpkins and
    buried in big-wigs
Why ask who ever yet saw money made out of a fat old
Jew or downright upright nutmegs out of a pine-knot.

To Marie Louise (Shew)

Not long ago, the writer of these lines,
In the mad pride of intellectuality,
Maintained "the power of words"—denied that ever
A thought arose within the human brain
Beyond the utterance of the human tongue:
And now, as if in mockery of that boast,
Two words—two foreign soft dissyllables—
Italian tones, made only to be murmured
By angels dreaming in the moonlit "dew
That hangs like chains of pearl on Hermon hill,"—
Have stirred from out the abysses of his heart,
Unthought-like thoughts that are the souls of thought,
Richer, far wilder, far diviner visions
Than even the seraph harper, Israfel,
(Who has "the sweetest voice of all God's creatures,")
Could hope to utter. And I! my spells are broken.
The pen falls powerless from my shivering hand.
With thy dear name as text, though hidden by thee,
I cannot write—I cannot speak or think—
Alas, I cannot feel; for 'tis not feeling,
This standing motionless upon the golden
Threshold of the wide-open gate of dreams,
Gazing, entranced, adown the gorgeous vista,
And thrilling as I see, upon the right,
Upon the left, and all the way along,
Amid empurpled vapors, far away
To where the prospect terminates—*thee only!*

Lines on Ale

Fill with mingled cream and amber
    I will drain that glass again.
Such hilarious visions clamber
    Through the chamber of my brain—
Quaintest thoughts—queerest fancies
    Come to life and fade away;
What care I how time advances?
    I am drinking ale today.

Eldorado

Gaily bedight,
A gallant knight,
In sunshine and in shadow,
Had journeyed long,
Singing a song,
In search of Eldorado.

But he grew old—
This knight so bold—
And o'er his heart a shadow
Fell as he found
No spot of ground
That looked like Eldorado.

And, as his strength
Failed him at length,
He met a pilgrim shadow—
"Shadow," said he,
"Where can it be—
This land of Eldorado?"

"Over the Mountains
Of the Moon,
Down the Valley of the Shadow,
Ride, boldly ride,"
The shade replied,—
"If you seek for Eldorado!"

The Bells

I

Heart he sledges with the bells—
Silver bells!
What a world of merriment their melody foretells!
How they tinkle, tinkle, tinkle,
In the icy air of night!
While the stars that oversprinkle
All the heavens, seem to twinkle
With a crystalline delight;
Keeping time, time, time,
In a sort of Runic rhyme,
To the tintinabulation that so musically wells
From the bells, bells, bells, bells,
Bells, bells, bells—
From the jingling and the tinkling of the bells.

II

Hear the mellow wedding bells,
Golden bells!
What a world of happiness their harmony foretells!
Through the balmy air of night
How they ring out their delight!—
From the molten-golden notes,
And all in tune,
What a liquid ditty floats
To the turtle-dove that listens, while she gloats
On the moon!
Oh, from out the sounding cells,
What a gush of euphony voluminously wells!
How it swells!

How it dwells
On the Future!—how it tells
Of the rapture that impels
To the swinging and the ringing
Of the bells, bells, bells,
Of the bells, bells, bells, bells,
Bells, bells, bells—
To the rhyming and the chiming of the bells!

III

Hear the loud alarum bells—
Brazen bells!
What a tale of terror, now, their turbulency tells!
In the startled ear of night
How they scream out their affright!
Too much horrified to speak,
They can only shriek, shriek,
Out of tune,
In a clamorous appealing to the mercy of the fire,
In a mad expostulation with the deaf and frantic fire,
Leaping higher, higher, higher,
With a desperate desire,
And a resolute endeavor
Now—now to sit or never,
By the side of the pale-faced moon.
Oh, the bells, bells, bells!
What a tale their terror tells
Of Despair!
How they clang, and clash, and roar!
What a horror they outpour
On the bosom of the palpitating air!
Yet the ear it fully knows,

By the twanging,
And the clanging,
How the danger ebbs and flows;
Yet the ear distinctly tells,
In the jangling,
And the wrangling,
How the danger sinks and swells,
By the sinking or the swelling in the anger of the
bells—
Of the bells—
Of the bells, bells, bells, bells,
Bells, bells, bells—
In the clamor and the clangor of the bells!

IV
Hear the tolling of the bells—
Iron bells!
What a world of solemn thought their monody
compels!
In the silence of the night,
How we shiver with affright
At the melancholy menace of their tone!
For every sound that floats
From the rust within their throats
Is a groan.
And the people—ah, the people—
They that dwell up in the steeple,
All alone,
And who tolling, tolling, tolling,
In that muffled monotone,
Feel a glory in so rolling
On the human heart a stone—

They are neither man nor woman—
They are neither brute nor human—
They are Ghouls:
And their king it is who tolls;
And he rolls, rolls, rolls,
Rolls
A pæan from the bells!
And his merry bosom swells
With the pæan of the bells!
And he dances, and he yells;
Keeping time, time, time,
In a sort of Runic rhyme,
To the pæan of the bells—
Of the bells:
Keeping time, time, time,
In a sort of Runic rhyme,
To the throbbing of the bells—
Of the bells, bells, bells—
To the sobbing of the bells;
Keeping time, time, time,
As he knells, knells, knells,
In a happy Runic rhyme,
To the rolling of the bells—
Of the bells, bells, bells—
To the tolling of the bells,
Of the bells, bells, bells, bells—
Bells, bells, bells—
To the moaning and the groaning of the bells.

To My Mother

Because I feel that, in the Heavens above,
    The angels, whispering to one another,
Can find, among their burning terms of love,
    None so devotional as that of "Mother,"
Therefore by that dear name I long have called you—
    You who are more than mother unto me,
And fill my heart of hearts, where Death installed you,
    In setting my Virginia's spirit free.
My mother—my own mother, who died early,
    Was but the mother of myself; but you
Are mother to the one I loved so dearly,
    And thus are dearer than the mother I knew
By that infinity with which my wife
    Was dearer to my soul than its soul-life.

For Annie

Thank Heaven! the crisis,
    The danger, is past,
And the lingering illness
    Is over at last—
And the fever called "Living"
    Is conquered at last.

Sadly, I know
    I am shorn of my strength,
And no muscle I move
    As I lie at full length—
But no matter!—I feel
    I am better at length.

And I rest so composedly,
    Now, in my bed,
That any beholder
    Might fancy me dead—
Might start at beholding me,
    Thinking me dead.

The moaning and groaning,
    The sighing and sobbing,
Are quieted now,
    With that horrible throbbing
At heart:—ah, that horrible,
    Horrible throbbing!

The sickness—the nausea—
    The pitiless pain—

Have ceased, with the fever
        That maddened my brain—
With the fever called "Living"
        That burned in my brain.

And oh! of all tortures
        That torture the worst
Has abated—the terrible
        Torture of thirst,
For the naphthaline river
        Of Passion accurst:—
I have drank of a water
        That quenches all thirst:—

Of a water that flows,
        With a lullaby sound,
From a spring but a very few
        Feet under ground—
From a cavern not very far
        Down under ground.

And ah! let it never
        Be foolishly said
That my room it is gloomy
        And narrow my bed—
For man never slept
        In a different bed;
And, to *sleep*, you must slumber
        In just such a bed.

My tantalized spirit
        Here blandly reposes,

Forgetting, or never
    Regretting, its roses—
Its old agitations
    Of myrtles and roses:

For now, while so quietly
    Lying, it fancies
A holier odor
    About it, of pansies—
A rosemary odor,
    Commingled with pansies—
With rue and the beautiful
    Puritan pansies.

And so it lies happily,
    Bathing in many
A dream of the truth
    And the beauty of Annie—
Drowned in a bath
    Of the tresses of Annie.

She tenderly kissed me,
    She fondly caressed,
And then I fell gently
    To sleep on her breast—
Deeply to sleep
    From the heaven of her breast.

When the light was extinguished,
    She covered me warm,
And she prayed to the angels
    To keep me from harm—

To the queen of the angels
    To shield me from harm.

And I lie so composedly,
    Now, in my bed,
(Knowing her love)
    That you fancy me dead—
And I rest so contentedly,
    Now, in my bed,
(With her love at my breast)
    That you fancy me dead—
That you shudder to look at me,
    Thinking me dead.

But my heart it is brighter
    Than all of the many
Stars in the sky,
    For it sparkles with Annie—
It glows with the light
    Of the love of my Annie—
With the thought of the light
    Of the eyes of my Annie.

A Dream Within a Dream

Take this kiss upon the brow!
And, in parting from you now,
Thus much let me avow—
You are not wrong, who deem
That my days have been a dream;
Yet if Hope has flown away
In a night, or in a day,
In a vision, or in none,
Is it therefore the less *gone?*
All that we see or seem
Is but a dream within a dream.
I stand amid the roar
Of a surf-tormented shore,
And I hold within my hand
Grains of the golden sand—
How few! yet how they creep
Through my fingers to the deep,
While I weep—while I weep!
O God! can I not grasp
Them with a tighter clasp?
O God! can I not save
One from the pitiless wave?
Is *all* that we see or seem
But a dream within a dream?

Annabel Lee

It was many and many a year ago,
    In a kingdom by the sea,
That a maiden there lived whom you may know
    By the name of ANNABEL LEE;
And this maiden she lived with no other thought
    Than to love and be loved by me.

I was a child and *she* was a child,
    In this kingdom by the sea,
But we loved with a love that was more than love—
    I and my ANNABEL LEE;
With a love that the wingèd seraphs of heaven
    Coveted her and me.

And this was the reason that, long ago,
    In this kingdom by the sea,
A wind blew out of a cloud, chilling
    My beautiful ANNABEL LEE;
So that her highborn kinsman came
    And bore her away from me,
To shut her up in a sepulchre
    In this kingdom by the sea.

The angels, not half so happy in heaven,
    Went envying her and me:—
Yes!—that was the reason (as all men know,
    In this kingdom by the sea)
That the wind came out of the cloud by night,
    Chilling and killing my ANNABEL LEE.

But our love it was stronger by far than the love
　　　Of those who were older than we—
　　　Of many far wiser than we—
And neither the angels in heaven above,
　　　Nor the demons down under the sea,
Can ever dissever my soul from the soul
　　　Of the beautiful ANNABEL LEE:—

For the moon never beams, without bringing me dreams
　　　Of the beautiful ANNABEL LEE;
And the stars never rise, but I feel the bright eyes
　　　Of the beautiful ANNABEL LEE:
And so, all the night-tide, I lie down by the side
Of my darling—my darling—my life and my bride,
　　　In the sepulchre there by the sea,
　　　In her tomb by the sounding sea.

To Zante

Fair isle, that from the fairest of all flowers,
 Thy gentlest of all gentle names dost take!
How many memories of what radiant hours
 At sight of thee and thine at once awake!
How many scenes of what departed bliss!
 How many thoughts of what entombed hopes!
How many visions of a maiden that is
 No more—no more upon thy verdant slopes!
No more! alas, that magical sad sound
 Transforming all! Thy charms shall please *no more*—
Thy memory *no more!* Accursed ground
 Henceforward I hold thy flower-enamelled shore,
O hyacinthine isle! O purple Zante!
 "Isola d'oro! Fior di Levante!"

Hymn

At morn—at noon—at twilight dim—
Maria! thou hast heard my hymn!
In joy and woe—in good and ill—
Mother of God, be with me still!
When the Hours flew brightly by,
And not a cloud obscured the sky,
My soul, lest it should truant be,
Thy grace did guide to thine and thee
Now, when storms of Fate o'ercast
Darkly my Present and my Past,
Let my future radiant shine
With sweet hopes of thee and thine!

Prose Poems

The Island of the Fay

Nullus enim locus sine genio est.
    Servius.

"*La musique*," says Marmontel, in those "Contes Moraux" which in all our translations we have insisted upon calling "Moral Tales," as if in mockery of their spirit—"*la musique est le seul des talens qui jouissent de lui-meme: tous les autres veulent des témoins.*" He here confounds the pleasure derivable from sweet sounds with the capacity for creating them. No more than any other *talent*, is that for music susceptible of complete enjoyment, where there is no second party to appreciate its exercise. And it is only in common with other talents that it produces *effects* which may be fully enjoyed in solitude. The idea which the *raconteur* has either failed to entertain clearly, or has sacrificed in its expression to his national love of *point*, is doubtless the very tenable one that the higher order of music is the most thoroughly estimated when we are exclusively alone. The proposition, in this form, will be admitted at once by those who love the lyre for its own sake, and for its spiritual uses. But there is one pleasure still within the reach of fallen mortality—and perhaps only one— which owes even more than does music to the accessory sentiment of seclusion. I mean the happiness experienced in the contemplation of natural scenery. In truth, the man who would behold aright the glory of God upon earth must in solitude behold that glory. To me, at least, the presence— not of human life only—but of life in any other form than that of the green things which grow upon the soil and are voiceless—is a stain upon the landscape—is at war with the genius of the scene. I love, indeed, to regard the dark valleys, and the gray rocks, and the waters that silently smile, and the forests that sigh in uneasy slumbers, and the proud watchful mountains that look down upon all—I love to regard these as themselves but the colossal members of one vast animate and sentient whole—a whole whose form (that of the sphere) is the most perfect and most inclusive of all; whose path is among associate planets; whose meek hand-maiden is the moon; whose mediate sovereign is the sun; whose life is eternity; whose thought is that of a God; whose enjoyment is knowledge; whose destinies are lost in immensity; whose cognizance of ourselves is akin with our own cognizance of the *animalculæ* which infest the brain—a being which we, in consequence, regard as purely inanimate and material, much in the same manner as these *animalculæ* must thus regard us.

Our telescopes and our mathematical investigations assure us on every hand—notwithstanding the cant of the more ignorant of the priesthood—that space, and therefore that bulk, is an important consideration in the eyes of the Almighty. The cycles in which the stars move are those best adapted for the evolution, without collision, of the greatest possible number of bodies. The forms of those bodies are accurately such as, within a given surface, to include the greatest possible amount of matter;—while the surfaces themselves are so disposed as to accommodate a denser population than could be accommodated on the same surfaces otherwise arranged. Nor is it any argument against bulk being an object with God, that space itself is infinite; for there may be an infinity of matter to fill it. And since we see clearly that the endowment of matter with vitality is a principle—indeed, as far as our judgments extend, the *leading* principle in the operations of Deity—it is scarcely logical to imagine it confined to the regions of the minute, where we daily trace it, and not extending to those of the august. As we find cycle within cycle without end, yet all revolving around one far-distant centre which is the Godhead, may we not analogically suppose, in the same manner, life within life, the less within the greater, and all within the Spirit Divine? In short, we are madly erring, through self-esteem, in believing man, in either his temporal or future destinies, to be of more moment in the universe than that vast "clod of the valley" which he tills and contemns, and to which he denies a soul for no more profound reason than that he does not behold it in operation.

These fancies, and such as these, have always given to my meditations among the mountains, and the forests, by the rivers and the ocean, a tinge of what the every-day world would not fail to term the fantastic. My wanderings amid such scenes have been many, and far-searching, and often solitary; and the interest with which I have strayed through many a dim deep valley, or gazed into the reflected heaven of many a bright lake, has been an interest greatly deepened by the thought that I have strayed and gazed *alone*. What flippant Frenchman was it who said, in allusion to the well known work of Zimmermann, that "*la solitude est une belle chose; mais il faut quelqu'un pour vous dire que la solitude est une belle chose*"? The epigram cannot be gainsaid; but the necessity is a thing that does not exist.

It was during one of my lonely journeyings, amid a far-distant region of mountain locked within mountain, and sad rivers and melancholy tarns writhing or sleeping within all—that I chanced upon a certain rivulet and island. I came upon them suddenly in the leafy June, and threw myself upon the turf, beneath the branches of an unknown odorous shrub, that I might doze as I contemplated the scene. I felt that thus only should I look upon it—such was the character of phantasm which it wore.

On all sides—save to the west, where the sun was about sinking—arose the verdant walls of the forest. The little river which turned sharply in its course, and was thus immediately lost to sight, seemed to have no exit from its prison, but to be absorbed by the deep green foliage of the trees to the east—while in the opposite quarter (so it appeared to me as I lay at length and glanced upward) there poured down noiselessly and continuously into the valley, a rich golden and crimson waterfall from the sunset fountains of the sky.

About midway in the short vista which my dreamy vision took in, one small circular island, profusely verdured, reposed upon the bosom of the stream.

> So blended bank and shadow there,
> That each seemed pendulous in air—

so mirror-like was the glassy water, that it was scarcely possible to say at what point upon the slope of the emerald turf its crystal dominion began.

My position enabled me to include in a single view both the eastern and western extremities of the islet; and I observed a singularly-marked difference in their aspects. The latter was all one radiant harem of garden beauties. It glowed and blushed beneath the eye of the slant sunlight, and fairly laughed with flowers. The grass was short, springy, sweet-scented, and Asphodel-interspersed. The trees were lithe, mirthful, erect—bright, slender, and graceful—of eastern figure and foliage, with bark smooth, glossy, and parti-colored. There seemed a deep sense of life and joy about all; and although no airs blew from out the Heavens, yet everything had motion through the gentle sweepings to and fro of innumerable butterflies, that might have been mistaken for tulips with wings.

The other or eastern end of the isle was whelmed in the blackest shade. A sombre, yet beautiful and peaceful gloom here pervaded all things. The trees were dark in color and mournful in form and attitude—wreathing themselves into sad, solemn, and spectral shapes, that conveyed ideas of mortal sorrow and untimely death. The grass wore the deep tint of the cypress, and the heads of its blades hung droop-ingly, and, hither and thither among it, were many small unsightly hillocks, low, and narrow, and not very long, that had the aspect of graves, but were not; although over and all about them the rue and the rosemary clambered. The shades of the trees fell heavily upon the water, and seemed to bury itself therein, impregnating the depths of the element with darkness. I fancied that each shadow, as the sun descended lower and lower, separated itself sullenly from the trunk that gave it birth, and thus became absorbed by the stream; while other shadows issued momently from the trees, taking the place of their predecessors thus entombed.

This idea, having once seized upon my fancy, greatly excited it, and I lost myself forthwith in reverie. "If ever island were enchanted," said I to myself, "this is it. This is the haunt of the few gentle Fays who remain from the wreck of the race. Are these green tombs theirs?—or do they yield up their sweet lives as mankind yield up their own? In dying, do they not rather waste away mournfully, rendering unto God little by little their existence, as these trees render up shadow after shadow, exhausting their substance unto dissolution? What the wasting tree is to the water that imbibes its shade, growing thus blacker by what it preys upon, may not the life of the Fay be to the death which engulfs it?"

As I thus mused, with half-shut eyes, while the sun sank rapidly to rest, and eddying currents careered round and round the island, bearing upon their bosom large, dazzling, white flakes of the bark of the sycamore—flakes which, in their multiform positions upon the water, a quick imagination might have converted into any thing it pleased—while I thus mused, it appeared to me that the form of one of those very Fays about whom I had been pondering, made its way slowly into the darkness from out the light at the western end of the island. She stood erect in a singularly fragile canoe, and urged it with the mere phantom of an oar. While within the influence of the lingering sunbeams, her attitude seemed indicative of joy—but sorrow deformed it as she passed within the shade. Slowly she glided along, and at length rounded the islet and re-entered the region of light. "The revolution which has just been made by the Fay," continued I, musingly, "is the cycle of the brief year of her life. She has floated through her winter and through her summer. She is a year nearer unto Death: for I did not fail to see that as she came into the shade, her shadow fell from her, and was swallowed up in the dark water, making its blackness more black."

And again the boat appeared, and the Fay; but about the attitude of the latter there was more of care and uncertainty, and less of elastic joy. She floated again from out the light, and into the gloom (which deepened momently) and again her shadow fell from her into the ebony water, and became absorbed into its blackness. And again and again she made the circuit of the island, (while the sun rushed down to his slumbers) and at each issuing into the light there was more sorrow about her person, while it grew feebler, and far fainter, and more indistinct; and at each passage into the gloom, there fell from her a darker shade, which became whelmed in a shadow more black. But at length, when the sun had utterly departed, the Fay, now the mere ghost of her former self, went disconsolately with her boat into the region of the ebony flood—and that she issued thence at all I cannot say—for darkness fell over all things, and I beheld her magical figure no more.

The Power of Words

Oinos.   Pardon, Agathos, the weakness of a spirit new-fledged with immortality!

Agathos.   You have spoken nothing, my Oinos, for which pardon is to be demanded. Not even here is knowledge a thing of intuition. For wisdom, ask of the angels freely, that it may be given!

Oinos.   But in this existence, I dreamed that I should be at once cognizant of all things, and thus at once happy in being cognizant of all.

Agathos.   Ah, not in knowledge is happiness, but in the acquisition of knowledge! In for ever knowing, we are for ever blessed; but to know all, were the curse of a fiend.

Oinos.   But does not The Most High know all?

Agathos.   That (since he is The Most Happy) must be still the *one* thing unknown even to Him.

Oinos.   But, since we grow hourly in knowledge, must not *at last* all things be known?

Agathos.   Look down into the abysmal distances!—attempt to force the gaze down the multitudinous vistas of the stars, as we sweep slowly through them thus—and thus—and thus! Even the spiritual vision, is it not at all points arrested by the continuous golden walls of the universe?—the walls of the myriads of the shining bodies that mere number has appeared to blend into unity?

Oinos.   I clearly perceive that the infinity of matter is no dream.

Agathos.   There are no dreams in Aidenn—but it is here whispered that, of this infinity of matter, the *sole* purpose is to afford infinite springs, at which the soul may allay the thirst *to know* which is for ever unquenchable within it—since to quench it, would be to extinguish the soul's self. Question me then, my Oinos, freely and without fear. Come! we will leave to the left the loud harmony of the Pleiades, and swoop outward from the throne into the starry meadows beyond Orion, where, for pansies and violets, and heart's-ease, are the beds of the triplicate and triple-tinted suns.

Oinos.   And now, Agathos, as we proceed, instruct me!— speak to me in the earth's familiar tones! I understand not what you hinted to me, just now, of the modes or of the methods of what, during mortality, we were accustomed to call Creation. Do you mean to say that the Creator is not God?

Agathos.   I mean to say that the Deity does not create.

Oinos.   Explain!

Agathos.   In the beginning only, he created. The seeming creatures which are now, throughout the universe, so perpetually springing into being, can only be considered as the mediate or indirect, not as the direct or immediate results of the Divine creative power.

Oinos.   Among men, my Agathos, this idea would be considered heretical in the extreme.

Agathos.   Among the angels, my Oinos, it is seen to be simply true.

Oinos.   I can comprehend you thus far—that certain operations of what we term Nature, or the natural laws, will, under certain conditions, give rise to that which has all the *appearance* of creation. Shortly before the final overthrow of the earth, there were, I well remember, many very successful experiments in what some philosophers were weak enough to denominate the creation of *animalculæ*.

Agathos.   The cases of which you speak were, in fact, instances of the secondary creation—and of the only species of creation which has ever been, since the first word spoke into existence the first law.

Oinos.   Are not the starry worlds that, from the abyss of non-entity, burst hourly forth into the heavens— are not these stars, Agathos, the immediate handiwork of the King?

Agathos. Let me endeavor, my Oinos, to lead you, step by step, to the conception I intend. You are well aware that, as no thought can perish, so no act is without infinite result. We moved our hands, for example, when we were dwellers on the earth, and, in so doing, we gave vibration to the atmosphere which engirdled it. This vibration was indefinitely extended, till it gave impulse to every particle of the earth's air, which thenceforward, and for ever, was actuated by the one movement of the hand. This fact the mathematicians of our globe well knew. They made the special effects, indeed, wrought in the fluid by special impulses, the subject of exact calculation—so that it became easy to determine in what precise period an impulse of given extent would engirdle the orb, and impress (for ever) every atom of the atmosphere circumambient. Retrograding, they found no difficulty, from a given effect, under given conditions, in determining the value of the original impulse. Now the mathematicians who saw that the results of any given impulse were absolutely endless—and who saw that a portion of these results were accurately traceable through the agency of algebraic analysis—who saw, too, the facility of the retrogradation—these men saw, at the same time, that this species of analysis itself, had within itself a capacity for indefinite progress— that there were no bounds conceivable to its advancement and applicability, except within the intellect of him who advanced or applied it. But at this point our mathematicians paused.

Oinos.   And why, Agathos, should they have proceeded?

Agathos.   Because there were some considerations of deep interest beyond. It was deducible from what they knew, that to a being of infinite understanding— one to whom the *perfection* of the algebraic analysis lay unfolded—there could be no difficulty in tracing every impulse given the air—and the ether through the air—to the remotest consequences at any even infinitely remote epoch of time. It is indeed demonstrable that every such impulse *given the air*, must, *in the end*, impress every individual thing that exists *within the universe;*—and the being of infinite understanding—the being whom we have imagined—might trace the remote undulations of the impulse—trace them upward and onward in their influences upon all particles of all matter—upward and onward for ever in their modifications of old forms—or, in other words, in *their creation of new*—until he found them reflected— unimpressive *at last*—back from the throne of the Godhead. And not only could such a being do this, but at any epoch, should a given result be afforded him—should one of these numberless comets, for example, be presented to his inspection—he could have no difficulty in determining, by the analytic retrogradation, to what original impulse it was due. This power of retrogradation in its absolute fulness and perfection—this faculty of referring at *all* epochs, *all* effects to *all* causes— is of course the prerogative of the Deity alone—but in every variety of degree, short of the absolute perfection, is the power itself exercised by the whole host of the Angelic Intelligences.

Oinos. But you speak merely of impulses upon the air.

Agathos. In speaking of the air, I referred only to the earth: but the general proposition has reference to impulses upon the ether—which, since it pervades, and alone pervades all space, is thus the great medium of *creation*.

Oinos. Then all motion, of whatever nature, creates?

Agathos. It must: but a true philosophy has long taught that the source of all motion is thought—and the source of all thought is—

Oinos. God.

Agathos. I have spoken to you, Oinos, as to a child, of the fair Earth which lately perished—of impulses upon the atmosphere of the earth.

Oinos. You did.

Agathos. And while I thus spoke, did there not cross your mind some thought of the *physical power of words*? Is not every word an impulse on the air?

Oinos. But why, Agathos, do you weep—and why, oh why do your wings droop as we hover above this fair star—which is the greenest and yet most terrible of all we have encountered in our flight? Its brilliant flowers look like a fairy dream—but its fierce volcanoes like the passions of a turbulent heart.

Agathos.   They *are!*—they *are!*—This wild star —it is now three centuries since, with clasped hands, and with streaming eyes, at the feet of my beloved —I spoke it—with a few passionate sentences—into birth. Its brilliant flowers *are* the dearest of all unfulfilled dreams, and its raging volcanoes *are* the passions of the most turbulent and unhallowed of hearts!

The Colloquy of Monos and Una

These things are in the future.
              Sophocles—*Antigone*

Una.   "Born again?"

Monos.   Yes, fairest and best beloved Una, "born again."
          These were the words upon whose mystical
          meaning I had so long pondered, rejecting the
          explanations of the priesthood, until Death itself
          resolved for me the secret.

Una.   Death!

Monos.   How strangely, sweet Una, you echo my words! I
          observe, too, a vacillation in your step—a joyous
          inquietude in your eyes. You are confused and
          oppressed by the majestic novelty of the Life
          Eternal. Yes, it was of Death I spoke. And here how
          singularly sounds that word which of old was
          wont to bring terror to all hearts—throwing a
          mildew upon all pleasures!

Una.   Ah, Death, the spectre which sate at all feasts! How
          often, Monos, did we lose ourselves in speculations
          upon its nature! How mysteriously did it act as a
          check to human bliss—saying unto it, "thus far,
          and no farther!" That earnest mutual love, my own
          Monos, which burned within our bosoms—how
          vainly did we flatter ourselves, feeling happy in

its first upspringing, that our happiness would strengthen with its strength! Alas, as it grew, so grew in our hearts the dread of that evil hour which was hurrying to separate us forever! Thus in time it became painful to love. Hate would have been mercy then.

Monos.   Speak not here of these griefs, dear Una—mine, mine forever now!

Una.   But the memory of past sorrow—is it not present joy? I have much to say yet of the things which have been. Above all, I burn to know the incidents of your own passage through the dark Valley and Shadow.

Monos.   And when did the radiant Una ask anything of her Monos in vain? I will be minute in relating all—but at what point shall the weird narrative begin?

Una.   At what point?

Monos.   You have said.

Una.   Monos, I comprehend you. In Death we have both learned the propensity of man to define the inde-finable. I will not say, then, commence with the moment of life's cessation—but commence with that sad, sad instant when, the fever having aban-doned you, you sank into a breathless and motionless torpor, and I pressed down your pallid eyelids with the passionate fingers of love.

Monos. One word first, my Una, in regard to man's general condition at this epoch. You will remember that one or two of the wise among our forefathers— wise in fact, although not in the world's esteem—had ventured to doubt the propriety of the term "improvement," as applied to the progress of our civilization. There were periods in each of the five or six centuries immediately preceding our dissolution, when arose some vigorous intellect, boldly contending for those principles whose truth appears now, to our disenfranchised reason, so utterly obvious—principles which should have taught our race to submit to the guidance of the natural laws, rather than attempt their control. At long intervals some masterminds appeared, looking upon each advance in practical science as a retro-gradation in the true utility. Occasionally the poetic intellect—that intellect which we now feel to have been the most exalted of all—since those truths which to us were of the most enduring importance could only be reached by that *analogy* which speaks in proof-tones to the imagination alone, and to the unaided reason bears no weight—occasionally did this poetic intellect proceed a step farther in the evolving of the vague idea of the philosophic, and find in the mystic parable that tells of the tree of knowledge, and of its forbidden fruit, death-producing, a distinct intimation that knowledge was not meet for man in the infant condition of his soul. And these men —the poets—living and perishing amid the scorn of the "utilitarians"—of rough pedants, who arrogated to themselves a title which could have been properly applied only to the scorned—these men, the poets, pondered piningly, yet not unwisely, upon the ancient days when our wants were not more simple than our enjoyments were keen—days when mirth was a word unknown, so solemnly deep-toned was happiness—holy, august, and blissful days, when blue rivers ran undammed, between hills unhewn, into far forest solitudes, primæval, odorous, and unexplored.

Yet these noble exceptions from the general misrule served but to strengthen it by opposition. Alas! we had fallen upon the most evil of all our evil days. The great "movement"—that was the cant term—went on: a diseased commotion, moral and physical. Art—the Arts—arose supreme, and, once enthroned, cast chains upon the intellect which had elevated them to power. Man, because he could not but acknowledge the majesty of Nature, fell into childish exultation at his acquired and still-increasing dominion over her elements. Even while he stalked a God in his own fancy, an infantine imbecility came over him. As might be supposed from the origin of his disorder, he grew infected with system, and with abstraction. He enwrapped himself in generalities. Among other odd ideas, that of universal equality gained ground; and in the face of analogy and of God—in despite of the loud warning voice of the laws of *gradation* so visibly pervading all things in Earth and Heaven—wild attempts at an omni-prevalent Democracy were made. Yet this evil sprang necessarily from the leading evil, Knowledge. Man could not both know and succumb. Meantime huge smoking cities arose, innumerable. Green leaves shrank before the hot breath of furnaces. The fair face of Nature was deformed as with the ravages of some loathsome disease. And methinks, sweet Una, even our slumbering sense of the forced and of the far-fetched might have arrested us here. But now it appears that we had worked out our own destruction in the perversion of our *taste*, or rather in the blind neglect of its culture in the schools. For, in truth, it was at this crisis that taste alone—that faculty which, holding a middle position between the pure intellect and the moral sense, could never safely have been disregarded—it was now that taste alone could have led us gently back to Beauty, to Nature, and to Life. But alas for the pure contemplative spirit and majestic intuition of Plato! Alas for the μουσικη which he justly regarded as an all-sufficient education for the soul! Alas for him and for it!—since both were most desperately needed, when both were most entirely forgotten or despised.

Pascal, a philosopher whom we both love, has said, how truly!—"*Que tout notre raisonnement se réduit à céder au sentiment;*" and it is not impossible that the sentiment of the natural, had time permitted it, would have regained its old ascendency over the harsh mathematical reason of the schools. But this thing was not to be. Prematurely induced by intemperance of knowledge, the old age of the world drew on. This the mass of mankind saw not, or, living lustily although unhappily, affected not to see. But, for myself, the Earth's records had taught me to look for widest ruin as the price of highest civilization. I had imbibed a prescience of our Fate from comparison of China the simple and enduring, with Assyria the architect, with Egypt the astrologer, with Nubia, more crafty than either, the turbulent mother of all Arts. In the history of these regions I met with a ray from the Future. The individual artificialities of the three latter were local diseases of the Earth, and in their individual overthrows we had seen local remedies applied; but for the infected world at large I could antic-ipate no regeneration save in death. That man, as a race, should not become extinct, I saw that he must be "born again."

And now it was, fairest and dearest, that we wrapped our spirits, daily, in dreams. Now it was that, in twilight, we discoursed of the days to come, when the Art-scarred surface of the Earth, having undergone that purification which alone could efface its rectangular obscenities, should clothe itself anew in the verdure and the mountain-slopes and the smiling waters of Paradise, and be rendered at length a fit dwelling-place for man:—for man the Death-purged—for man to whose now exalted intellect there should be poison in knowledge no more—for the redeemed, regenerated, blissful, and now immortal, but still for the *material*, man.

Una.	Well do I remember these conversations, dear Monos; but the epoch of the fiery overthrow was not so near at hand as we believed, and as the corruption you indicate did surely warrant us in believing. Men lived; and died individually. You yourself sickened, and passed into the grave; and thither your constant Una speedily followed you. And though the century which has since elapsed, and whose conclusion brings up together once more, tortured our slumbering senses with no impatience of duration, yet, my Monos, it was a century still.
Monos.	Say, rather, a point in the vague infinity. Unquestionably, it was in the Earth's dotage that I died. Wearied at heart with anxieties which had their origin in the general turmoil and decay, I succumbed to the fierce fever. After some few days of pain, and many of dreamy delirium replete with ecstasy, the manifestations of which you mistook for pain, while I longed but was impotent to undeceive you—after some days there came upon me, as you have said, a breathless and motionless torpor; and this was termed *Death* by those who stood around me.

Words are vague things. My condition did not deprive me of sentience. It appeared to me not greatly dissimilar to the extreme quiescence of him, who, having slumbered long and profoundly, lying motionless and fully prostrate in a midsummer noon, begins to steal slowly back into consciousness, through the mere sufficiency of his sleep, and without being awakened by external disturbances.

I breathed no longer. The pulses were still. The heart had ceased to beat. Volition had not departed, but was powerless. The senses were unusually active, although eccentrically so—assuming often each other's functions at random. The taste and the smell were inextricably confounded, and became one sentiment, abnormal and intense. The rose-water with which your tenderness had moistened my lips to the last, affected me with sweet fancies of flowers—fantastic flowers, far more lovely than any of the old Earth, but whose prototypes we have here blooming around us. The eyelids, transparent and bloodless, offered no complete impediment to vision. As volition was in abeyance, the balls could not roll in their sockets—but all objects within the range of the visual hemisphere were seen with more or less distinctness; the rays which fell upon the external retina, or into the corner of the eye, producing a more vivid effect than those which struck the front or interior surface. Yet, in the former instance, this effect was so far anomalous that I appreciated it only as *sound*—sound sweet or discordant as the matters presenting themselves at my side were light or dark in shade—curved or angular in outline. The hearing, at the same time, although excited in degree, was not irregular in action—estimating real sounds with an extravagance of precision, not less than of sensibility. Touch had undergone a modification more peculiar. Its impressions were tardily received, but pertinaciously retained, and resulted always in the highest physical pleasure. Thus the pressure of your sweet fingers upon my eyelids, at first only recognised through vision, at length, long after their removal, filled my whole being with a sensual delight immeasurable. I say with a sensual delight. *All* my perceptions were purely sensual. The materials furnished the passive brain by the senses were not in the least degree wrought into shape by the deceased understanding. Of pain there was some little; of pleasure there was much; but of moral pain or pleasure none at all. Thus your wild sobs floated into my ear with all their mournful cadences, and were appreciated in their every variation of sad tone; but they were soft musical sounds and no more; they conveyed to the extinct reason no intimation of the sorrows which gave them birth; while large and constant tears which fell upon my face, telling the bystanders of a heart which broke, thrilled every fibre of my frame with ecstasy alone. And this was in truth the *Death* of which these bystanders spoke reverently, in low whispers—you, sweet Una, gaspingly, with loud cries.

They attired me for the coffin—three or four dark figures which flitted busily to and fro. As these crossed the direct line of my vision they affected me as *forms*; but upon passing to my side their images impressed me with the idea of shrieks, groans, and, other dismal expressions of terror, of horror, or of woe. You alone, habited in a white robe, passed in all directions musically about me.

The day waned; and, as its light faded away, I became possessed by a vague uneasiness—an anxiety such as the sleeper feels when sad real sounds fall continuously within his ear—low distant bell-tones, solemn, at long but equal intervals, and commingling with melancholy dreams. Night arrived; and with its shadows a heavy discomfort. It oppressed my limbs with the oppression of some dull weight, and was palpable. There was also a moaning sound, not unlike the distant reverberation of surf, but more continuous, which, beginning with the first twilight, had grown in strength with the darkness. Suddenly lights were brought into the rooms, and this reverberation became forthwith interrupted into frequent unequal bursts of the same sound, but less dreary and less distinct. The ponderous oppression was in a great measure relieved; and, issuing from the flame of each lamp (for there were many), there flowed unbrokenly into my ears a strain of melodious monotone. And when now, dear Una, approaching the bed upon which I lay outstretched, you sat gently by my side, breathing odor from your sweet lips, and pressing them upon my brow, there arose tremulously within my bosom, and mingling with the merely physical sensations which circumstances had called forth, a something akin to sentiment itself— a feeling that, half appreciating, half responded to your earnest love and sorrow; but this feeling took no root in the pulseless heart, and seemed indeed rather a shadow than a reality, and faded quickly away, first into extreme quiescence, and then into a purely sensual pleasure as before.

And now, from the wreck and the chaos of the usual senses, there appeared to have arisen within me a sixth, all perfect. In its exercise I found a wild delight—yet a delight still physical, inasmuch as the understanding had in it no part. Motion in the animal frame had fully ceased. No muscle quivered; no nerve thrilled; no artery throbbed. But there seemed to have sprung up in the brain, that of which no words could convey to the merely human intelligence even an indistinct conception. Let me term it a mental pendulous pulsation. It was the moral embodiment of man's abstract idea of Time. By the absolute equalization of this movement—or of such as this—had the cycles of the firmamental orbs themselves, been adjusted. By its aid I measured the irregularities of the clock upon the mantel, and of the watches of the attendants. Their tickings came sonorously to my ears. The slightest deviations from the true proportion—and these deviations were omni-prævalent—affected me just as violations of abstract truth were wont, on earth, to affect the moral sense. Although no two of the timepieces in the chamber struck the individual seconds accurately together, yet I had no difficulty in holding steadily in mind the tones, and the respective momentary errors of each. And this—this keen, perfect self-existing sentiment of *duration*—this sentiment existing (as man could not possibly have conceived it to exist) independently of any succession of events—this idea—this sixth sense, upspringing from the ashes of the rest, was the first obvious and certain step of the intemporal soul upon the threshold of the temporal Eternity.

It was midnight; and you still sat by my side. All others had departed from the chamber of Death. They had deposited me in the coffin. The lamps burned flickeringly; for this I knew by the tremulousness of the monotonous strains. But, suddenly these strains diminished in distinctness and in volume. Finally they ceased. The perfume in my nostrils died away. Forms affected my vision no longer. The oppression of the Darkness uplifted itself from my bosom. A dull shot like that of electricity pervaded my frame, and was followed by total loss of the idea of contact. All of what man has termed sense was merged in the sole consciousness of entity, and in the one abiding sentiment of duration. The mortal body had been at length stricken with the hand of the deadly *Decay*.

Yet had not all of sentience departed; for the consciousness and the sentiment remaining supplied some of its functions by a lethargic intuition. I appreciated the direful change now in operation upon the flesh, and, as the dreamer is sometimes aware of the bodily presence of one who leans over him, so, sweet Una, I still dully felt that you sat by my side. So, too, when the noon of the second day came, I was not unconscious of those movements which displaced you from my side, which confined me within the coffin, which deposited me within the hearse, which bore me to the grave, which lowered me within it, which heaped heavily the mould upon me, and which thus left me, in blackness and corruption, to my sad and solemn slumbers with the worm.

And here, in the prison-house which has few secrets to disclose, there rolled away days and weeks and months; and the soul watched narrowly each second as it flew, and, without effort, took record of its flight—without effort and without object.

A year passed. The consciousness of *being* had grown hourly more indistinct, and that of mere *locality* had, in great measure, usurped its position. The idea of entity was becoming merged in that of *place*. The narrow space immediately surrounding what had been the body was now growing to be the body itself. At length, as often happens to the sleeper (by sleep and its world alone is *Death* imaged) —at length, as sometimes happened on Earth to the deep slumberer, when some flitting light half startled him into awaking, yet left him half enveloped in dreams—so to me, in the strict embrace of the *Shadow*, came *that* light which alone might have had power to startle—the light of enduring *Love*. Men toiled at the grave in which I lay darkling. They up-threw the damp earth. Upon my mouldering bones there descended the coffin of Una. And now again all was void. That nebulous light had been extinguished. That feeble thrill had vibrated itself into quiescence. Many *lustra* had supervened. Dust had returned to dust. The worm had food no more. The sense of being had at length utterly departed, and there reigned in its stead— instead of all things—dominant and perpetual—the autocrats *Place* and *Time*. For *that* which *was not*—for that which had no form—for that which had no thought—for that which had no sentience—for that which was soundless, yet of which matter formed no portion—for all this nothingness, yet for all this immortality, the grave was still a home, and the corrosive hours, co-mates.

The Conversation of Eiros and Charmion

I will bring fire to thee.
Euripides—*Andromache*

Eiros.   Why do you call me Eiros?

Charmion. So henceforward will you always be called. You must forget, too, my earthly name, and speak to me as Charmion.

Eiros.   This is indeed no dream!

Charmion. Dreams are with us no more;—but of these mysteries anon. I rejoice to see you looking life-like and rational. The film of the shadow has already passed from off your eyes. Be of heart, and fear nothing. Your allotted days of stupor have expired, and tomorrow I will myself induct you into the full joys and wonders of your novel existence.

Eiros.   True—I feel no stupor—none at all. The wild sickness and the terrible darkness have left me, and I hear no longer that mad, rushing, horrible sound, like the "voice of many waters." Yet my senses are bewildered, Charmion, with the keenness of their perception of *the new.*

Charmion. A few days will remove all this;—but I fully understand you, and feel for you. It is now ten earthly years since I underwent what you undergo—yet the remembrance of it hangs by me still. You have now suffered all of pain, however, which you will suffer in Aidenn.

Eiros. In Aidenn?

Charmion. In Aidenn.

Eiros. O God!—pity me, Charmion!—I am over-burthened with the majesty of all things—of the unknown now known—of the speculative Future merged in the august and certain Present.

Charmion. Grapple not now with such thoughts. Tomorrow we will speak of this. Your mind wavers, and its agitation will find relief in the exercise of simple memories. Look not around, nor forward—but back. I am burning with anxiety to hear the details of that stupendous event which threw you among us. Tell me of it. Let us converse of familiar things, in the old familiar language of the world which has so fearfully perished.

Eiros. Most fearfully, fearfully!—this is indeed no dream.

Charmion. Dreams are no more. Was I much mourned, my Eiros?

Eiros. Mourned, Charmion?—oh, deeply. To that last hour of all, there hung a cloud of intense gloom and devout sorrow over your household.

Charmion. And that last hour—speak of it. Remember that, beyond the naked fact of the catastrophe itself, I know nothing. When, coming out from among mankind, I passed into Night through the Grave—at that period, if I remember aright, the calamity which overwhelmed you was utterly unanticipated. But, indeed, I knew little of the speculative philosophy of the day.

Eiros. The individual calamity was, as you say, entirely unanticipated; but analogous misfortunes had been long a subject of discussion with astronomers. I need scarce tell you, my friend, that, even when you left us, men had agreed to understand those passages in the most holy writings which speak of the final destruction of all things by fire, as having reference to the orb of the earth alone. But in regard to the immediate agency of the ruin, speculation had been at fault from that epoch in astronomical knowledge in which the comets were divested of the terrors of flame. The very moderate density of these bodies had been well established. They had been observed to pass among the satellites of Jupiter, without bringing about any sensible alteration either in the masses or in the orbits of these secondary planets. We had long regarded the wanderers as vapory creations of inconceivable tenuity, and as altogether incapable of doing injury to our substantial globe, even in the event of contact. But contact was not in any degree dreaded; for the elements of all the comets were accurately known. That among them we should look for the agency of the threatened fiery destruction had been for many years considered an inadmissible idea. But wonders and wild fancies had been, of late days, strangely rife among mankind; and, although it was only with a few of the ignorant that actual apprehension prevailed, upon the announcement by astronomers of a new comet, yet this announcement was generally received with I know not what of agitation and mistrust.

The elements of the strange orb were immediately calculated, and it was at once conceded by all observers that its path, at perihelion, would bring it into very close proximity with the earth. There were two or three astronomers of secondary note, who resolutely maintained that a contact was inevitable. I cannot very well express to you the effect of this intelligence upon the people. For a few short days they would not believe an assertion which their intellect, so long employed among worldly considerations, could not in any manner grasp. But the truth of a vitally important fact soon makes its way into the understanding of even the most stolid. Finally, all men saw that astronomical knowledge lied not, and they awaited the comet. Its approach was not, at first, seemingly rapid; nor was its appearance of very unusual character. It was of a dull red, and had little perceptible train. For seven or eight days we saw no material increase in its apparent diameter, and but a partial alteration in its color. Meantime, the ordinary affairs of men were discarded, and all interest absorbed in a growing discussion, instituted by the philosophic, in respect to the cometary nature. Even the grossly ignorant aroused their sluggish capacities to such considerations. The learned *now* gave their intellect—their soul—to no such points as the allaying of fear, or to the sustenance of loved theory. They sought—they panted for right views. They groaned for perfected knowledge. *Truth* arose in the purity of her strength and exceeding majesty, and the wise bowed down and adored.

That material injury to our globe or to its inhabitants would result from the apprehended contact, was an opinion which hourly lost ground among the wise; and the wise were now freely permitted to rule the reason and the fancy of the crowd. It was demonstrated that the density of the comet's *nucleus* was far less than that of our rarest gas; and the harmless passage of a similar visitor among the satellites of Jupiter was a point strongly insisted upon, and which served greatly to allay terror. Theologists, with an earnestness fear-enkindled, dwelt upon the biblical prophecies, and expounded them to the people with a directness and simplicity of which no previous instance had been known. That the final destruction of the earth must be brought about by the agency of fire, was urged with a spirit that enforced every where conviction; and that the comets were of no fiery nature (as all men now knew) was a truth which relieved all, in a great measure, from the apprehension of the great calamity foretold. It is noticeable that the popular prejudices and vulgar errors in regard to pestilences and wars—errors which were wont to prevail upon every appearance of a comet—were now altogether unknown. As if by some sudden convulsive exertion, reason had at once hurled superstition from her throne. The feeblest intellect had derived vigor from excessive interest.

What minor evils might arise from the contact were points of elaborate question. The learned spoke of slight geological disturbances, of probable alterations in climate, and consequently in vegetation; of possible magnetic and electric influences. Many held that no visible or perceptible effect would in any manner be produced. While such discussions were going on, their subject gradually approached, growing larger in apparent diameter, and of a more brilliant lustre. Mankind grew paler as it came. All human operations were suspended.

There was an epoch in the course of the general sentiment when the comet had attained, at length, a size surpassing that of any previously recorded visitation. The people now, dismissing any lingering hope that the astronomers were wrong, experienced all the certainty of evil. The chimerical aspect of their terror was gone. The hearts of the stoutest of our race beat violently within their bosoms. A very few days suffered, however, to merge even such feelings in sentiments more unendurable. We could no longer apply to the strange orb any *accustomed* thoughts. Its histor-ical attributes had disappeared. It oppressed us with a hideous *novelty* of emotion. We saw it not as an astronomical phenomenon in the heavens, but as an incubus upon our hearts, and a shadow upon our brains. It had taken, with unconceivable rapidity, the character of a gigantic mantle of rare flame, extending from horizon to horizon.

Yet a day, and men breathed with greater freedom. It was clear that we were already within the influ-ence of the comet; yet we lived. We even felt an unusual elasticity of frame and vivacity of mind. The exceeding tenuity of the object of our dread was apparent; for all heavenly objects were plainly visible through it. Meantime, our vegetation had perceptibly altered; and we gained faith, from this predicted circumstance, in the foresight of the wise. A wild luxuriance of foliage, utterly unknown before, burst out upon every vegetable thing.

Yet another day—and the evil was not altogether upon us. It was now evident that its nucleus would first reach us. A wild change had come over all men; and the first sense of *pain* was the wild signal for general lamentation and horror. The first sense of pain lay in a rigorous construction of the breast and lungs, and an insufferable dryness of the skin. It could not be denied that our atmosphere was radically affected; the conformation of this atmos-phere and the possible modifications to which it might be subjected, were now the topics of discussion. The result of investigation sent an electric thrill of the intensest terror through the universal heart of man.

It had been long known that the air which encircled us was a compound of oxygen and nitrogen gases, in the proportion of twenty-one measures of oxygen and seventy-nine of nitrogen in every one hundred of the atmosphere. Oxygen, which was the principle of combustion, and the vehicle of heat, was absolutely necessary to the support of animal life, and was the most powerful and energetic agent in nature. Nitrogen, on the contrary, was incapable of supporting either animal life or flame. An unnatural excess of oxygen would result, it had been ascertained, in just such an elevation of the animal spirits as we had latterly experienced. It was the pursuit, the extension of the idea, which had engendered awe. What would be the result of a *total extraction of the nitrogen*? A combustion irresistible, all-devouring, omni-prevalent, immediate;— the entire fulfillment, in all their minute and terrible details, of the fiery and horror-inspiring denunciations of the prophecies of the Holy Book.

Why need I paint, Charmion, the now disenchained frenzy of mankind? That tenuity in the comet which had previously inspired us with hope, was now the source of the bitterness of despair. In its impalpable gaseous character we clearly perceived the consummation of Fate. Meantime a day again passed—bearing away with it the last shadow of Hope. We gasped in the rapid modification of the air. The red blood bounded tumultuously through its strict channels. A furious delirium possessed all men; and with arms rigidly outstretched towards the threatening heavens, they trembled and shrieked aloud. But the nucleus of the destroyer was now upon us;—even here in Aidenn I shudder while I speak. Let me be brief—brief as the ruin that overwhelmed. For a moment there was a wild lurid light alone, visiting and penetrating all things. Then—let us bow down, Charmion, before the excessive majesty of the great God!—then, there came a shouting and pervading sound, as if from the mouth itself of HIM; while the whole incumbent mass of ether in which we existed, burst at once into a species of intense flame, for whose surpassing brilliancy and all-fervid heat even the angels in the high Heaven of pure knowledge have no name. Thus ended all.

Shadow—a Parable

Yea! though I walk through the valley of the *Shadow*.
Psalm of David.

Ye who read are still among the living; but I who write
shall have long since gone my way into the region of shadows.
For indeed strange things shall happen, and secret things be
known, and many centuries shall pass away, ere these memo-
rials be seen of men. And, when seen, there will be some
to disbelieve and some to doubt, and yet a few who will
find much to ponder upon in the characters here graven
with a stylus of iron.

The year had been a year of terror, and of feeling more
intense than terror for which there is no name upon the
earth. For many prodigies and signs had taken place, and
far and wide, over sea and land, the black wings of the
Pestilence were spread abroad. To those, nevertheless, cunning
in the stars, it was not unknown that the heavens wore an
aspect of ill; and to me, the Greek Oinos, among others, it
was evident that now had arrived the alternation of that
seven hundred and ninety-fourth year when, at the entrance
of Aries, the planet Jupiter is enjoined with the red ring of
the terrible Saturnus. The peculiar spirit of the skies, if I
mistake not greatly, made itself manifest, not only in the
physical orb of the earth, but in the souls, imaginations, and
meditations of mankind.

Over some flasks of the red Chian wine, within the walls
of a noble hall, in a dim city called Ptolemais, we sat, at

night, a company of seven. And to our chamber there was no entrance save by a lofty door of brass: and the door was fashioned by the artisan Corinnos, and, being of rare workmanship, was fastened from within. Black draperies, likewise in the gloomy room, shut out from our view the moon, the lurid stars, and the peopleless streets—but the boding and the memory of Evil, they would not be so excluded. There were things around us and about of which I can render no distinct account—things material and spiritual—heaviness in the atmosphere—a sense of suffocation—anxiety—and, above all, that terrible state of existence which the nervous experience when the senses are keenly living and awake, and meanwhile the powers of thought lie dormant. A deadweight hung upon us. It hung upon our limbs—upon the household furniture—upon the goblets from which we drank; and all things were depressed, and borne down thereby—all things save only the flames of the seven iron lamps which illumined our revel. Uprearing themselves in tall slender lines of light, they thus remained burning all pallid and motionless; and in the mirror which their lustre formed upon the round table of ebony at which we sat, each of us there assembled beheld the pallor of his own countenance, and the unquiet glare in the downcast eyes of his companions. Yet we laughed and were merry in our proper way—which was hysterical; and sang the songs of Anacreon—which are madness; and drank deeply—although the purple wine reminded us of blood. For there was yet another tenant of our chamber in the person of young Zoilus. Dead, and at full length he lay, enshrouded;—the genius and the demon of the scene. Alas! he bore no portion in our mirth, save that his countenance, distorted with the plague, and his eyes in which Death had but half extinguished the fire of the pestilence, seemed to take such an interest in our merriment as the dead may haply take in the merriment of those who are to die. But although I, Oinos, felt that the eyes of the departed were upon me, still I forced myself not to perceive the bitterness of their expression, and gazing down steadily into the depths of the ebony mirror, sang with a loud and sonorous voice the songs of the son of Teios. But gradually my songs they ceased, and their echoes, rolling afar off among the sable draperies of the chamber, became weak, and undistinguishable, and so faded away. And lo! from among those sable draperies, where the sounds of the song departed, there came forth a dark and undefiled shadow—a shadow such as the moon, when low in heaven, might fashion from the figure of a man: but it was the shadow neither of man nor of God, nor of any familiar thing. And, quivering awhile among the draperies of the room, it at length rested in full view upon the surface of the door of brass. But the shadow was vague, and formless, and indefinite, and was the shadow neither of man nor God—neither God of Greece, nor God of Chaldæa, nor any Egyptian God. And the shadow rested upon the brazen doorway, and under the arch of the entablature of the door, and moved not, nor spoke any word, but there became stationary and remained. And the door whereupon the shadow rested was, if I remember aright, over against the feet of the young Zoilus enshrouded. But we, the seven there assembled, having seen the shadow as it came out from among the draperies, dared not steadily behold it, but cast down our eyes, and gazed continually into the depths of the mirror of ebony. And at length I, Oinos, speaking some low words, demanded of the shadow its dwelling and its appellation. And the shadow answered, "I am Shadow, and my dwelling is near to the Catacombs of Ptolemais, and hard by those dim plains of Helusion which border upon the foul Charonian canal." And then did we, the seven, start from our seats in horror, and stand trembling, and shuddering, and aghast: for the tones in the voice of the shadow were not the tones of any one being, but of a multitude of beings, and, varying in their cadences from syllable to syllable, fell duskily upon our ears in the well remembered and familiar accents of many thousand departed friends.

Silence—a Fable

The mountain pinnacles slumber; valleys, crags, and caves are silent.

"Listen to me," said the Demon, as he placed his hand upon my head. "The region of which I speak is a dreary region in Libya, by the borders of the river Zäire. And there is no quiet there, nor silence.

"The waters of the river have a saffron and sickly hue; and they flow not onwards to the sea, but palpitate forever and forever beneath the red eye of the sun with a tumultuous and convulsive motion. For many miles on either side of the river's oozy bed is a pale desert of gigantic water-lilies. They sigh one unto the other in that solitude, and stretch towards the heaven their long and ghastly necks, and nod to and fro their everlasting heads. And there is an indistinct murmur which cometh out from among them like the rushing of subterrene water. And they sigh one unto the other.

"But there is a boundary to their realm—the boundary of the dark, horrible, lofty forest. There, like the waves about the Hebrides, the low underwood is agitated continually. But there is no wind throughout the heaven. And the tall primeval trees rock eternally hither and thither with a crashing and mighty sound. And from their high summits, one by one, drop everlasting dews. And at the roots, strange poisonous flowers lie writhing in perturbed slumber. And overhead, with a rustling and loud noise, the gray clouds rush westwardly forever until they roll, a cataract, over the fiery wall of the horizon. But there is no wind throughout the heaven.

And by the shores of the river Zäire there is neither quiet nor silence.

"It was night, and the rain fell; and, falling, it was rain, but, having fallen, it was blood. And I stood in the morass among the tall lilies, and the rain fell upon my head—and the lilies sighed one unto the other in the solemnity of their desolation.

"And, all at once, the moon arose through the thin ghastly mist, and was crimson in color. And mine eyes fell upon a huge gray rock which stood by the shore of the river, and was lighted by the light of the moon. And the rock was gray and ghastly, and tall,—and the rock was gray. Upon its front were characters engraven in the stones; and I walked through the morass of water-lilies, until I came close unto the shore, that I might read the characters upon the stone. But I could not decypher them. And I was going back into the morass when the moon shone with a fuller red, and I turned and looked again upon the rock and upon the characters;—and the characters were Desolation.

"And I looked upwards, and there stood a man upon the summit of the rock; and I hid myself among the water-lilies that I might discover the action of the man. And the man was tall and stately in form, and was wrapped up from his shoulders to his feet in the toga of old Rome. And the outlines of his figure were indistinct—but his features were the features of a deity; for the mantle of the night, and of the mist, and of the moon, and of the dew, had left uncovered the features of his face. And his brow was lofty with thought, and his eye wild with care; and, in the few furrows upon his cheek I read the fables of sorrow, and weariness, and disgust with mankind, and a longing after solitude.

"And the man sat upon the rock, and leaned his head upon his hand, and looked out upon the desolation. He looked down into the low unquiet shrubbery, and up into the tall primeval trees, and up higher at the rustling heaven, and into the crimson moon. And I lay close within shelter of the lilies, and observed the actions of the man. And the man trembled in the solitude;—but the night waned, and he sat upon the rock.

"And the man turned his attention from the heaven, and looked out upon the dreary river Zäire, and upon the yellow ghastly waters, and upon the pale legions of the water-lilies. And the man listened to the sighs of the water-lilies, and to the murmur that came up from among them. And I lay close within my covert and observed the actions of the man. And the man trembled in the solitude;—but the night waned, and he sat upon the rock.

"Then I went down into the recesses of the morass, and waded afar in among the wilderness of the lilies, and called unto the hippopotami which dwelt among the fens in the recesses of the morass. And the hippopotami heard my call, and came, with the behemoth, unto the foot of the rock, and roared loudly and fearfully beneath the moon. And I lay close within my covert and observed the actions of the man. And the man trembled in the solitude;—but the night waned, and he sat upon the rock.

"Then I cursed the elements with the curse of tumult; and a frightful tempest gathered in the heaven, where, before, there had been no wind. And the heaven became livid with the violence of the tempest—and the rain beat upon the head of the man—and the floods of the river came down— and the river was tormented into foam—and the water-lilies shrieked within their beds—and the forest crumbled before the wind—and the thunder rolled—and the lightning fell— and the rock rocked to its foundation. And I lay close within my covert and observed the actions of the man. And the man trembled in the solitude;—but the night waned, and he sat upon the rock.

"Then I grew angry and cursed, with the curse of silence, the river, and the lilies, and the wind, and the forest, and the heaven, and the thunder, and the sighs of the water-lilies. And they became accursed, and were still. And the moon ceased to totter up its pathway to heaven—and the thunder died away—and the lightning did not flash—and the clouds hung motionless—and the waters sunk to their level and remained—and the trees ceased to rock—and the water-lilies sighed no more—and the murmur was heard no longer from among them, nor any shadow of sound throughout the vast illimitable desert. And I looked upon the characters of the rock, and they were changed;—and the characters were Silence.

"And mine eyes fell upon the countenance of the man, and his countenance was wan with terror. And, hurriedly, he raised his head from his hand, and stood forth upon the rock and listened. But there was no voice throughout the vast illimitable desert, and the characters upon the rock were Silence. And the man shuddered, and turned his face away, and fled afar off, in haste, so that I beheld him no more."

Now there are fine tales in the volumes of the Magi—in the iron-bound, melancholy volumes of the Magi. Therein, I say, are glorious histories of the Heaven, and of the Earth, and of the mighty Sea—and of the Genii that over-ruled the sea, and the earth, and the lofty heaven. There was much lore, too, in the sayings which were said by the Sybils; and holy, holy things were heard of old by the dim leaves that trembled around Dodona—but, as Allah liveth, that fable which the Demon told me as he sat by my side in the shadow of the tomb, I hold to be the most wonderful of all! And as the Demon made an end of his story, he fell back within the cavity of the tomb and laughed. And I could not laugh with the Demon, and he cursed me because I could not laugh. And the lynx which dwelleth forever in the tomb, came out therefrom, and lay down at the feet of the Demon, and looked at him steadily in the face.

Index

Poems

Prose Poems